It's All About Bob(bie)

STRATEGIES FOR WINNING WITH YOUR EMPLOYEES

Foreword by
Jennifer A. Chatman, PhD
Paul J. Cortese Distinguished Professor of Management,
Haas School of Business,
University of California, Berkeley

First printed November 2015

The paper used in this book meets the minimum requirements
of the American National Standard for Information Services
ANSI Z39.48-1984 (Permanence of Paper for Printed Library Materials)

Text: Dante MT
Display: Rotis Serif, Semi Serif, and Sans Serif

ISBN 978-0-9799554-3-3 (print version)
ISBN 978-0-9799554-4-0 (e-version)
Printed and bound in the United States of America.

Kronos Incorporated
297 Billerica Road
Chelmsford, MA 01824
Ph: 978.250.9800 Fx: 978.367.5900

Table of Contents

FOREWORD

Jennifer A. Chatman, PhD
Paul J. Cortese Distinguished Professor of Management,
Haas School of Business, University of California, Berkeley

Workplace behavioral research aims to help us understand group conflict, collaboration, and cooperation. Focusing largely on how people interact with each other on the job, how norms form and dictate behavior, and how this behavior influences long-term firm performance, researchers in social psychology and organizational behavior have observed something often overlooked in organizations — that productivity, engagement, and clarity in purpose are all related. Studies show employees who are more satisfied and have a clearer understanding about their organization's strategic goals are more productive, more helpful in accomplishing their organization's strategic aspirations, and have more impact in forming valuable and lasting relationships with customers.

So, what is the common denominator of organizations that stand out in ensuring happy, satisfied, productive, and engaged employees? What *is* it that is embraced in their corporate norms that serves the best interests of customers, the satisfaction of employees, and the future progress and continued success of these organizations? Studies show today's high-performing organizations excel at:

1. Communicating that company culture, one that is strategically relevant, strong, and adaptive is top focus; and taking steps to make it so (e.g., Chatman et al., 2014, Chatman, 2013).

2. Listening to their employees and providing with ways to offer honest and anonymous feedback.

3. Asking their employees how happy they are on a regular basis, and

how clear they are about the organization's strategic direction.
4. Providing employees with the development opportunities and tools
they need to do their best work.

Organizations need to recognize the importance of adaptability in successfully motivating and inspiring employees as well as consistently meeting strategic objectives. Currently, I'm conducting a study with colleagues which will be the first to identify the underlying mechanisms of how leader influence styles create a lasting culture — one that can either foster or kill innovation depending on the leader's approach. A leader who is high on the influence style trustworthiness, for example, is more likely to create a culture that emphasizes integrity while a leader who uses openness as an influence style is more likely to create an innovative culture. In contrast, for lower status leaders, their own influence approach may be less broadly characteristic of the culture of the organization over which they have responsibility. We are currently analyzing the data we have collected from 135 senior leaders.

Corporate cultures that achieve all four points listed above in ensuring happy, satisfied, productive, and engaged employees show wide agreement in strongly held norms. In essence, these organizations parse culture into content and consensus and create relationships driven by missions of higher purpose and/or of changing the world. Their employees derive a higher purpose from their work, and are more inclined to stay. Further, studies show these organizations not only use — but stretch — their employee skills, often assigning employees new challenges to enhance their level of work satisfaction and sustain a high-quality workforce.

Today's workforce represents a spectrum of generations that vary in work motivation, values, styles, habits, needs, and strengths. Workforce diversity exists on other attributes as well. For example, as a result of recent demographic shifts in the U.S. workforce women outnumber men for the first time in history. Ethnic, geographic, and cross cultural variation is at an all-time high. As such, organizations need to find ways to foster a balance between inspiring diverse teams with collective goals while also valuing the distinctions among people that allow for creativity and innovation to flourish.

Specific behaviors and perceptions in the workplace — including gender biases, prejudices, political correctness, and individual processing, categorizing, and interpreting of information — are increasingly studied to see how and to what level they influence workplace performance. Diverse work groups are complex and some of the research results are surprising and counter intuitive. For example, I recently conducted a study (Goncalo, Chatman, Duguid, & Kennedy, 2015) that showed how emphasizing the group norm of political correctness did not constrain performance, as many believed it would, but instead enabled diverse groups to be more creative by reducing uncertainty about how to interact with group members who differed in their demographic profile.

The pages that follow in this collection are written by some of today's leading experts in leveraging workforce efficiencies and organizational culture change through leadership, management, recruitment, technology, and employee satisfaction. Each chapter offers insights and perspectives in creating and sustaining a winning workforce. Of significance, this anthology serves to remind us that workforce planning, previously the domain of only futurists, is now within our reach — in the domain of operational effectiveness — to fuel bottom line success.

INTRODUCTION

Joyce O'Donnell Maroney
Director, The Workforce Institute, Kronos Incorporated

I experienced the worst and best customer service experiences of my life from competing companies on the same day a few years ago. My widowed father's Alzheimer's disease had progressed to the point where he could no longer remain in an independent living apartment in his over-60 community. We made the decision to move him into a memory care unit. He would be safe, but no longer free to come and go. We were extremely anxious about this move, knowing that he would be unhappy about having his freedom curtailed.

In order to make his transition as easy as possible, we painted his room in familiar colors and decorated it with family pictures. Six weeks in advance of the move, I ordered a mattress set from a well-known national chain. The sales guy was great and absolutely guaranteed that the mattress would be delivered on time. Several days before the scheduled delivery, I got a call confirming the details. The night before, they called again to confirm the delivery details. Great customer service, right?

Except that thirty minutes before the mattress was due to be delivered, I got a call informing me that the delivery would be delayed — for about 5 days. Got the picture? Elderly parent with dementia, moving day, extreme emotional anxiety under any circumstances — and now Dad won't have a bed. Can we just buy a different bed? Nope. No inventory. My son, overhearing my phone conversation with the completely unhelpful mattress company employee, said, "That's the first time in my life I've heard you go to Defcon Five."

In desperation, I began calling alternative sellers in my area asking for a mattress set to be delivered within three hours. The first couple I spoke with were polite in offering their regrets, but not their help. I kept calling — and that's when the best customer experience of my life began. I recounted my story to "Bob," a sympathetic store manager. He told me to hang tight, and that he'd call me back within 30 minutes. Within fifteen minutes, he'd found a mattress set that could be delivered by 5 p.m. I thanked him for his efforts and reiterated that I needed it by 3 p.m. — the outside edge of when I could delay my Dad's move. I knew the minute he walked into a new setting he'd want to lay down on his bed, and no bed would mean utter confusion and agitation for him. Bob said he'd do his best. And he did. He found another mattress set and arranged for delivery before 3 p.m. Dad walked into a completely furnished apartment, his bed made with familiar bedding.

The most surprising thing of all? The store in question wasn't even Bob's home store. He was filling in for a co-worker for the day.

Great organizations are defined by the extent to which their brand promise translates into the rewarding experiences that we have when we interact with them. Thinking about companies like Disney, Apple, The Container Store, and USAA make most of us reflect on positive experiences we've had there, experiences we'd like to have again — just like my Bob experience. When we encounter their brand message, we think "that's right" rather than "yeah, right."

How do they do it? They create cultures where employees are trained to succeed, rewarded for great customer service, and provided with opportunities to grow in their careers. Communication about the company vision and objectives is clear, frequent, and delivered through employee-friendly channels. They view their employees as key drivers of their success, not just fungible costs to be managed. When we interact with these organizations, we feel the difference.

In my role at Kronos, I am responsible for our voice of the customer program, listening for issues that diminish our customer satisfaction and then driving responses to those issues. I network with a lot of leaders of these programs at other companies. As Director of the Workforce Institute, I'm regularly exposed to ideas about what makes a great place to work. What I've realized over time is that the companies with the greatest customer satisfaction are also highly likely to show up on "great place to work"

lists. The organizations that hire, develop, and retain the Bobs of this world are the ones that outsell and out-service their competitors.

The most recent Gallup State of the Workplace survey tells us, though, that only 13% of employees are truly engaged in their jobs. As consumers, we're frequently disappointed by the quality of the goods we purchase and the poor customer service we receive from the vendors or service providers we encounter. Many organizations aren't meeting the needs of their customers or their workers. This same research shows that for-profit companies with highly engaged workforces outperform their competitors by 147% in earnings per share. So why isn't there a lot more focus among leaders on improving employee engagement?

Most employers want to hold on to their great employees and do right by their customers, but the economic pressures they face can get in the way. It's daunting to build a profitable organization that does right by its employees and its customers — but it's not impossible. From the smallest organizations to the largest, there are proven principles that can drive employee engagement, create happier customers, and enhance performance.

One of my colleagues at Kronos, Charlie Dewitt, came up with a framework a few years ago to describe the continuum of employer attitudes and investments in their employees that we call the Workforce Maturity Curve.

The Workforce Maturity Curve is a way to think about the continuum of employer attitudes toward their employees, as well as the incremental returns they gain as they increase their investment in their employees. Over the years, serving thousands of organizations worldwide, we've seen firsthand the success of our customers who invest in employees as a key driver of success vs. an expense to be managed. There are four recognizable evolutionary stages to this view of organizational maturity.

Phase 1: Standardize, Streamline, and Simplify to Unburden Your Workforce

This is the first and foundational step on the path. The organization actively seeks to unburden their employees from inefficiency and low value tasks. They take the time to clearly articulate goals, streamline the processes that impact those goals, and automate low-value work so that their people can work on meaningful things. Policies are clear and consistently enforced. Accountability and auditability create a more democratic work environment.

Phase 2: Put the Best Team on the Field

At this stage of maturity, organizations are hiring the candidates who are most likely to be successful in the job based on their skills, experience and culture fit. In hourly environments, they are scheduling people based on business needs and employee skills and preferences. They incorporate their human resource needs into their strategic planning — identifying the people skills required for success in the short and the long term.

Phase 3: Help Your People Do Their Best Every Day

This stage is about creating a truly engaged workforce, one filled with the kind of people who'll go the extra mile to achieve your organization's objectives. In his book *Drive*,[1] Daniel Pink describes three key drivers of employee engagement:

1. *Autonomy* — the desire to direct our own lives.
2. *Mastery* — the urge to get better and better at something that matters.
3. *Purpose* — the yearning to do what we do in the service of something larger than ourselves.

When these three drivers are aligned, your people know what the mission is, they know what to do to impact success, and it's meaningful to them when they are successful because they are recognized and rewarded.

Phase 4: Continuous Improvement and Innovation

The world around our organizations doesn't stand still. New challenges and opportunities can stress even the best organizations. And the best organizations understand that their people are their key sustainable competitive advantage. Money, assets, patents, brand, product, channels... all of that can be replicated with enough effort and money. Top talent who believe in your mission and are willing to do their best for you are irreplaceable.

READING THIS BOOK AND JOINING THE CONVERSATION

The objective of this book is to reveal how organizations can have happy employees, loyal customers, and better results than ever before. Think of this book as a how-to-guide for creating that virtuous cycle in your workplace — for everybody from the frontline workforce to the Chief Executive Officer. Our authors are all recognized experts in the world of human capital management. Their advice in this book is focused on how you can make changes in your organization that will help you achieve greater sustainable advantage through your employees.

Each chapter begins and ends with a reflection on how the advice offered can impact an individual employee (Bob or Bobbie) for the better. You can read this book from start to finish, or dip into individual chapters according to your needs and interests.

We'd love to hear your ideas, too. This book is a starting point, not an exhaustive catalogue, of ideas for succeeding with your employees. If you have an idea you'd like to share, comment at www.workforceinstitute.org or tweet your idea to @WF_Institute.

ENDNOTES

1   Daniel H. Pink, *Drive: The Surprising Truth about What Motivates Us*, (New York, NY: Riverhead Books, 2009).

Section 1

STANDARDIZE, STREAMLINE, AND SIMPLIFY TO UNBURDEN YOUR WORKFORCE

Bob loves working in retail, but stressful days or nights —
depending on his shift — have him thinking of a career
change or at least a switch to another retailer. "I'm a
people-person, and I love fashion, so retail is perfect for
me. You know the saying the *clothes make the man* — or
woman? I got into retail to help people feel good about
themselves in their clothes. I love how looking good makes
me feel, so I want to help my customers enjoy that same
feeling." Bob's frustration stems from the volume swings
in a retail day. "It seems like we're either so busy we can't
help all the customers needing assistance, or it's so dead
the other associates and I are standing around staring at
each other. Neither extreme is very enjoyable."

CHAPTER ONE

Aligning Business Process with Organizational Goals

Mark Wales, MBA
Vice President, Global Workforce Management

> *"It is not about what you did yesterday,*
> *not even about what you did today,*
> *but what you dream of for tomorrow."*
>
> — Ralph Lauren, 2014

Executing Your Dreams through Your People

In New York, I listened to a friend who was starting a new wine bar. Like many new business owners, he was struggling to find the funding and the right people to bring his dream alive. In the midst of all the pressure, the conflicting priorities and the competing drains on his funds, he took his fledgling team on a spa day. Why was this such a priority for him?

Soon after hearing this story, I listened to the owner of a small New York restaurant with a very loyal local clientele explain why he doesn't expand: He does not believe that he could find and train additional staff that would host his customers in the way he would. He worries they would fail to consistently deliver on his values: how he welcomes, services, and satisfies his customers' expectations.

What these small business owners have is not only a vision of what their business should be, but also a fundamental belief that their dream has to be executed in the right way to be successful and sustainable. To do this, they must bring their strategy and execution together through their people.

For most organizations, large or small, dreams and visions become a reality *through* employees. Many of the most admired new and established retailers have a very special relationship with their employees, and this relationship translates directly into the way their employees treat their customers — which in turn helps these companies outperform their competition. While not a new concept, developing this kind of special relationship with employees remains a tough challenge for many retailers who see their payroll as their largest controllable cost. They struggle to find the right language and framework to uncover the true value of their employees, as well as how to design and build the right organization and processes to support their organizational goals.

Building That Special Relationship with Your Employees

In London in the early 1900s, John Spaden Lewis had a very different view of how employees should be treated compared to his contemporary competition. He saw his father's success coming from the value his father offered to his customers on Bond Street. However, John believed that even greater suc-

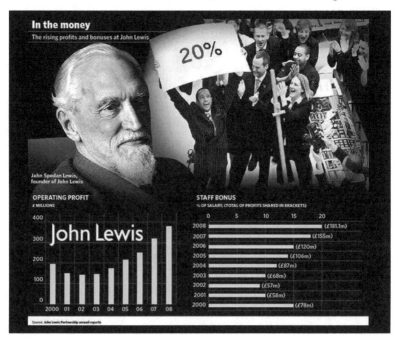

cess would come if you offered similar value to your employees as well. He took a very forward-thinking approach and introduced shortened work days, a staff committee, and holiday pay. In 1920, he introduced the idea of profit sharing and, not long after, turned the company into a partnership with the employees. Today, the John Lewis Partnership continues to be a very successful retailer with 93,800 partners. It continues to distinguish itself by the value it offers to customers and the way it cares for its partners. In his own words, you can hear John Lewis explain his philosophy in a 1957 BBC recording which is found on the John Lewis Partnership website.

In the United States, we see established retailers like The Container Store, Whole Foods, and Wegmans; newer retailers such as Zappos; and emerging retailers like Warby Parker, all operate with the firm belief that their relationship with their staff is key to their success. This is not just a European or North American trend. Success stories can be found in emerging markets as well, as in the case of Chili Beans, a sunglasses company from Brazil. Chili Beans' relationship with their employees has reached a level where some of their employees are actually tattooing the company logo on their bodies.

Sadly, too many retailers continue to see their employees as a "controllable cost." By categorizing payroll as a cost you are having the wrong conversation. Just like product development or real estate, your employees are an investment that you should be passionate about. If small business owners can recognize the vital role their employees play in their success, why do so many big businesses fail to remember? Why are they not asking the right questions about how to invest in their payroll and how can they maximize their return on that investment?

If you look closely at the companies that outperform their peers, often they are recognized for the way they take individual or different approaches to organizing around their employees. They are seeking to find the right balance of employee engagement, productivity, and customer service to match their company values.

For example, Disney designates staff as actors, and trains them on how to "own the moment" with their guests; Zappos is known for their flat management structure and exceptional employee perks; Costco and The Container Store make HR the responsibility of all managers; Whole Foods relies on team interviewing and touts salary transparency; Southwest Airlines emphasizes team empowerment and simplicity; and Wegmans is known for their peer rewards for service. Recently we have seen signs of change across other major chains as well, for example Walmart has been improving pay, conditions, and even store temperatures in an attempt to bring a greater focus on their employee experience.

The Importance of Workforce Management

The emergence of workforce management as a true management discipline is the evolution of the art and science of how to invest in your employee experience to impact your customer experience, which in turn will drive your sales and profitability.

Workforce management has evolved into a holistic discipline that brings together the people, processes, and technology from across the organization to balance the needs of the customer and the needs of the employee to maximize sales and profitability. For many, the basic tenet of workforce management is:

"Right People, Right Place, Right Time"

This is a simple but very powerful message that you will hear many retailers and service providers speak to when they discuss their strategy for investing in workforce management. This principle has been built on the thinking that aligning your staffing to the needs of your customers is the key to success in the retail or services industry. However, those that have tried to live by this ideal have soon realized that that there is another dimension that transcends this basic tenet, and leads to a more mature tenet:

"Right People, Right Place, Right Time, Right Behaviors"

This concept has evolved from the real-life experience of creating the perfect payroll allocation and schedule, and ending up with results that don't match expectations. Sitting in front of a Chief Executive Officer or Chief Financial Officer and having to explain why an additional investment in payroll isn't a linear equation that brings guaranteed increases in sales and profitability can be a tough experience. While having to have this conversation doesn't mean the strategy isn't right, it does call into question how you execute that strategy. Did you do everything you could to set your employees up for success?

By looking at how your employees behave towards your customers, each other, and your business partners, you get closer to understanding what drives success. How your staff behaves really comes down to how they align to your core values:

- Do they embody what your brand actually stands for?
- Have you created the culture to nurture your values?
- Have you empowered your employees to deliver your values?
- Have you designed your processes to support the needs of your employees?
- Are they engaged and giving that extra discretionary effort?

To be successful, all parts of the organization must be aligned and focused on the importance of workforce management. They must be willing to be accountable for their contribution to the customer and employee experience. Having the right conversation in the right language can lead to a different view of how to achieve success.

Entrepreneur, author, and Airbnb Head of Global Hospitality Chip Conley explains in his TED Talk how he developed his belief that every single employee is key to his customers' experiences, and that if those experiences are memorable, his customers will return more often, driving the success and profitability of his organization. Chip went on to grow Joie De Vivre into the second largest U.S. boutique hotel chain and has become a recognized authority for his approach and thoughts.

Redesigning Your Operations to Support Your Employees

Modern workforce management requires a holistic approach where you must redesign your operational processes in creative ways. This isn't a new approach: in the 1990s an executive team from the U.K.-based grocery chain, Tesco, returned from a U.S. visit believing that their organization had lost the "smell of the customer." At the time, Tesco believed their strength came from operational efficiency, with tight controls on payroll, and with traditional layered steps to authorize many operational processes such as customer returns. In a bold and industry-changing move, the then Chief Executive Officer, Sir Ian Maclaurin, made a radical decision. He empowered his staff to focus on the customers and what they expected and needed. In the grocery industry, this was an innovative move that shocked both the organization and the industry. What was required here was not just a change in values at an executive level, but a way to translate and execute those values as part of the customer experience. While the goal was to increase sales and profitability, Tesco realized that it had to change the customer experience and made their staff the focal point by empowering them to directly address the customer's needs and expectations.

To ensure that customers understood the change, Tesco began a very successful advertising campaign called "Every little helps," which showcased this new focus on the customer experience. In one ad, a customer returns a fish because it doesn't look happy. Another highlighted the fact that if a line exceeded five people a new check out would be opened. Ironically, the ad campaign garnered more recognition for its creative success than the operational strategy behind it. But in actuality, Tesco had to totally redefine its operations, eliminating many of the established controls and allowing managers and staff on the floor to make decisions in real-time to honor publicly advertised commitments to customers to return products, to take customers to the product they wanted, and to open more checkouts when queues exceeded five people.

Ultimately, Tesco rebuilt their employee experience to deliver a superior customer experience leading to a revenue increase from £8B to £17.4B and an increase in market share from 9.1% to 15.4%, with Tesco overtaking Sainsbury's to become the market leader in 1995. Furthermore, having developed credibility with its customer base, Tesco was able to broaden its offerings and move into new products and services, continuing to fuel growth for the organization. This approach flew in the face of traditional thinking that payroll was a controllable cost and proved that a one-dimensional view that ignores customers and employees will not maximize sales and profitability.

Right People, Right Place, Right Time, Right Behaviors
This story is still playing out in many new and older retailers and service

providers. What is required is a focus on the four key areas of Right People, Right Place, Right Time and Right Behaviors.

- Right people
  — looking at your
  hiring, training,
  and retention.

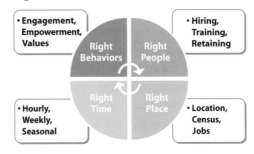

- Right place —
  understanding
  which locations
  and jobs need to
  be staffed.

- Right time — forecasting when you need staffing based on your seasonal, weekly, daily, and hourly needs.

- Right behaviors — building your structure and processes to empower your staff to make the right decisions when interacting with customers, colleagues, and business partners.

While you may develop programs, initiatives, and incentives to address each of these areas separately, the fundamental goal is to achieve the right balance across all four of the key areas. If you are not hiring the right people with the right availability, then you will not be able to focus on the right place or right time. If you are not retaining your staff, then the constant turnover will mean higher numbers of untrained or partially trained staff trying to deliver your customer experience. In all roles, across management, sales floor, and the back of the house, it takes time to learn the culture, the product, the processes, and the systems. New staff are rarely able to consistently deliver on your customer expectations and so degrade the customer experience. This turnover is the carbon monoxide of retail — a silent killer. It is rarely accounted for or measured in terms of productivity or customer experience. Once you begin to have the conversation in these terms, payroll is not a controllable cost but instead a fundamental investment in how to achieve the goals of the organization.

Hiring and retaining the right people are the first steps to building your foundation. Next is scheduling them at the right place and the right time to maximize their ability to be successful. Finally, the hardest part is creating the right culture and processes to sustain the cascading decisions that are made at every level of the organization to ensure that every customer interaction matches the values of the organization.

For Zappos, this has meant an adoption of the "holacracy" approach to management: embracing new ideas and ways to match their processes to the needs of the customer. This includes experimenting with free market scheduling in their call center, and rewarding staff for selecting high customer demand periods that may be unpopular.

With Disney, it means empowering employees to "own the moment" during each of the 11 billion possible interactions between a customer and a Disney park. Rather than talking about CRM, "Customer Relationship Management," Disney talks about CMR, "Customer Managed Relationship." This language shift encourages a different mentality for all those cascading decisions making up a customer's experience.

In a recent review, Deloitte noted that Southwest Airlines, "one of the top 20 rated employers in 2014, has honed simplicity and empowerment in its business model. The company focuses heavily on employee empowerment in its management training, letting the local team (the airplane crew) make all the decisions they need to run safely, on time, and on budget. The company also works hard to keep its entire business simple: Southwest uses a single airplane model (Boeing 737) and common boarding and reservations processes for every flight. The company has celebrated more than 40 years of profitability and continues to score among the highest in customer satisfaction year after year."

A common theme in all of these successful organizations is having the faith to empower employees to make decisions in real-time that can positively affect the quality of the customer experience, giving staff the ultimate reward: the ability to be successful in what they do.

What we must do is build the right organization, the right processes, and the right systems to deliver both the customer and employee experiences that reflect our values. Let's take a look at how the process of cascading decisions works in a prescriptive traditional retail environment and in a more progressive empowered organization. Which of these more closely resembles your organization?

	Traditional Retail or Services	Empowered Organization
Payroll: **Investment or cost?**	Payroll is constrained as a controllable cost. Stores may be understaffed and payroll is seen as a primary lever to support expense control and meet short-term financial goals.	Payroll is invested dynamically to match customer demand and may include over-staffing during the slow seasons to support employee engagement and reduce turnover.
Customer Focus: **Customer or Task focused?**	Employees are held accountable for task work and sales. This typically leads to a more narrow set of tasks and owned responsibilities. With formal oversight and controls, bureaucracy and KPIs are based around sales in a channel, productivity, and/or task work.	Employees are empowered to focus on the customer experience, which requires a blend of task work and sales with the in-the-moment ability to do what is necessary to satisfy the customer. This could mean showing them to a product, helping them to their car, encouraging an online purchase, or any other variable customer-focused action.
Effectiveness: **Adding or removing cost?**	Employees must get manager approvals for returns, free shipping, alterations, or any other discretionary decisions. This leads to delays and frustration with the customer, the employee, and the manager. Often it adds no value to the process, lowers the likelihood of a return visit from the customer, and increases the risk of dis-engagement for the customer, employee, and manager.	Employees are empowered to respond immediately to customer needs turning a problem into an opportunity to win back the customer. This frees the manager to spend more time interacting with customers and coaching in the moment with employees. This increases customer satisfaction, reducing manager and employee turnover.
Efficiency: **Simple or complex?**	Custom ordering processes are convoluted, manually intensive, error prone, complex, and require extensive knowledge and experience of product combinations and vendor processes. This results in employees spending the majority of their time following up on orders and paperwork instead of interacting with the customer.	Processes are simple and intuitive, and stock and product information is accurate, easily accessible, and supported by training materials and digital assets. Employees can build orders interactively with customers and spend the majority of their time engaging the customer and ensuring that the experience is memorable.

You will have many examples that are relevant to your organization but these examples show the differing ways to look at your organization and processes. What is important here is that the way you build your culture and processes has a direct impact on the level of engagement of your employees. Ask yourself:

Do your employees give that extra discretionary effort and make the right decision to satisfy your customer, or does the culture and the processes restrict and constrain them to a point where they are making the wrong decisions?

Are your employees more worried about completing task work at the expense of the customer experience or, worse, are they not even worried about the customer experience and are part of the disengaged workforce?

In 2012, a Gallup study showed that 63% of employees are not engaged and a further 24% are actively disengaged. This means only 13% of employees are giving that extra discretionary effort that is often required to really deliver a memorable customer experience. Are your structure and processes designed to maximize employee engagement or are you creating barriers and obstacles that prevent employee engagement and hurt the customer experience?

Changing the Conversation

If your organization is using the wrong language by focusing on payroll as a controllable cost, if you are not designing your processes around both the customer and the employee, and therefore failing to maximize your investment in payroll, where do you start in changing the conversation? Try starting with the tenet:

"Right People, Right Place, Right Time, Right Behaviors"

Use this lens to examine all of your decisions, processes, and policies to try to align the whole organization from the executives to backroom staff. Help everyone to find the right balance for your organization between the needs of the customers and employees. Make sure that your managers are spending their time interacting with the customers and coaching the employees. Move your investment in labor away from the task work and target the time that really impacts the customer experience. Make it everyone's responsibility in the organization to ensure that customers have memorable experiences that will bring them back, time after time. This investment of time, focus, and resources has proven to be a successful key strategic investment for many of the world's most admired retailers and service providers.

After a heart-to-heart with his manager, Lisa, Bob decided to stay on to see how the store changes she described would work out. After a few months, Bob was really enjoying work again, and the store was beating its numbers. "It's so much *steadier* now," said Bob. "Since

our schedules were adjusted and we were cross-trained to know the merchandise in more departments, the shifts fly by, *and* they're not so stressful. Sure, we still get crazy rushes, but they're much less frequent than they used to be. Now we're better able to spend the time to help our customers get what they really want. I don't feel rushed, and they don't feel rushed. It's a better experience for everyone. We're always busy now, but it's a *good busy*."

Growing up, Bobbie was one of the best gamers in her neighborhood. Part of the reason was because she was one of the best gamers in her household with four brothers! Whether it was snowboarding on the TV game console or the wizarding game on Dad's PC, Bobbie was fiercely competitive, and remains so today. Now, the working mom juggles college classes and her job at a manufacturing facility while always keeping her 7-year-old daughter, Nicole, her top priority. Bobbie likes her job, and her brother works at the same company, but she's barely making ends meet and is frustrated that she's rarely called upon when a shift opens up after a co-worker calls out. "It seems my manager only calls her favorites. I always ask and make sure she knows when I'm available, but she never calls me and it's not fair that just a couple people get all the extra shifts. With the holidays coming up, we could all use the extra money."

CHAPTER TWO

Unburden Your Employees through the Technology Advantage

Bob Clements
Senior Vice President, Strategy, Axsium Group

For nearly 2.6 million years, human beings have used technology to improve productivity and quality of life. Stone Age technology helped our prehistoric ancestors develop from nomadic tribes to civilized societies. During the Agricultural Age, technology produced food surpluses which allowed the development of specialized jobs that allowed even faster advances in technology. The Industrial Revolution spawned mass production and arguably has had the largest impact on human beings and our society of any prior event. Our lifespans have increased, fast transportation makes travel beyond our hometown easy, instantaneous long-distance communication connects people from around the world, and global trade brings goods and services from around the world to our doorstep. Many of the things we take for granted today are Industrial Age technologies.

But progress has a price, and that price has often been labor. Throughout our history, when labor got expensive, technology was introduced that used capital and resources to increase worker output. This brought labor costs down and, eventually, left people out of work. In the Agriculture Age, advances in food production technology meant the world needed fewer farmers, which led to the migration of unemployed farmers to cities seeking work. There, they found jobs in factories. As industrial technology advanced, factories became more efficient and fewer factory jobs were required.

Today, most developed nations live in the Information Age. Our economies are driven less and less by mass production and more and more by knowledge and information. Technology will continue to be used to automate increasingly more production tasks, wringing labor out of the process. However, smart employers are starting to look at technology in a different way. Smart employers are looking to technology to empower their people, unburdening their employees from low-value work and letting them focus more time on high-value activities. Doing so becomes a win-win-win: Customers benefit from high quality products and services; Employees benefit from more interesting and rewarding work, important drivers of employee engagement; And, finally, the employer benefits because employees are happier, making it easier to recruit and retain talent — which ultimately leads to happier customers, in turn driving better corporate performance.

This chapter focuses on how smart employers are using technology to unburden their employees and improve employee engagement. In this chapter, we'll describe technology trends that are affecting our employees and three emerging technologies that can help improve their engagement. First, let's focus on frontline managers, the important role they play in employee engagement, and how technology can help them find time to be more effective.

CREATING MORE TIME FOR ENGAGEMENT

The relationship an employee has with his or her direct manager is perhaps the most important driver of engagement. Gallup says the manager's or supervisor's position allows him or her to take the lead in establishing a culture that values behaviors that influence whether someone's expectations are clear, and whether he or she feels cared about (Harder, Schmidt, Argawal, & Plowman, 2013). A 2014 survey conducted by Netsurvey with Bain & Company found 87% of employees that were "promoters" of their company also highly rated their direct-line supervisor (Kaufman, Markey, Burton, & Azzarello, 2013).

However, across all industries, managers spend more time on administration than with frontline employees. McKinsey & Company found that managers spend 30 to 60% of their time on administration and meetings and 10 to 50% of their time on non-managerial tasks such as problem solving, special projects, or direct customer service, while they spend only 10 to 40% of their time with frontline employees (De Smet, McGurk, & Vinson, 2009).

Therefore, the most important thing we can do to increase employee engagement is to increase the amount of time that our managers spend with their teams. Once we do that, we can ask whether the manager has the skills to provide the necessary coaching. Otherwise, without the time to coach, the question of ability is moot.

You cannot expect your managers to find time on their own. This approach is neither practical nor efficient. They did not create the administrative tasks they are being asked to do. They cannot prioritize what is important to their managers and those above them without guessing or guidance from the top. Moreover, left to their own devices, each manager will likely solve the problem their own way which leads to inconsistent operations. Finally, if we try to put the solution on our managers, each manager will spend time trying to solve the same problem which creates redundant, wasteful work. Instead, it is the responsibility of our managers' managers and other leaders to help off-load low-value administrative tasks and provide time for high-value management tasks.

A big opportunity for time savings is by automating with people-related administration. Scheduling, handling time-off requests, managing attendance, approving timesheets, and managing payroll can chew up hours of a manager's week. At Axsium Group, we are often asked to help organizations assess how much time their managers spend on these activities. It is not unusual for managers to spend four to 16 hours each week on these chores and, in extreme cases, managers may spend up to 32 hours per week on these essential but relatively-low value-added projects.

Workforce Management (WFM) and Human Capital Management (HCM) systems that automate and streamline these processes can significantly reduce the amount of time that managers spend on these tasks. Based on our experience at Axsium Group, organizations can help managers cut the amount of time they spend on these types of functions by half. While the time savings can be dramatic, small savings can have a big impact on an organization. One large apparel retailer was able to justify their investment in a WFM system under the basic premise that they could save one hour per week for every manager and redeploy that hour in either a customer-facing or employee-facing activity.

Of course, automating these tasks provides more benefit than just making time for employee engagement. For the manager, automation eliminates the drudgery of administration. This makes their job more enjoyable and keeps them happy. Automation also helps increase accuracy. Without automation, these key functions need to be done manually, which almost always introduces errors into the process. Also, in many cases, the automated system can produce a better result than the manager could on his or her own.

Consider what happens when an employee calls in sick. After getting the sick call, the manager should take several steps. First, he or she should determine if a replacement needs to be called in the given current business environment. If a replacement is needed, the manager should look at who is available to fill that shift based on skills, certifications, availability, potential overtime, and individual productivity. He or she should start calling each employee — starting with the best fit — to see who can fill the shift. Instead, most managers just assume they need to fill the shift and quickly call one or two "go-to" employees who they always call in these situations because they know they will be happy to pick-up the extra shifts. They take this shortcut because it is easier and takes less time than doing it the right way.

A modern WFM system can automate this process. Once a manager identifies an employee is sick, the system can help the manager understand if a replacement is needed by showing the impact of the employee's absence on the planned workload. Then, if a replacement is required, the WFM system can automatically identify a list of potential replacements that meet certain availability, skill, cost, and/or productivity requirements, and then send text messages to these candidates to see which one is available to work. The employees can reply to the text to pick-up the shift. This entire process can take just a few minutes, considerably faster than even the shortcut.

For the workforce, automating these activities increases transparency and fairness, concepts that are critical factors to employee engagement. In the above example, the WFM system helps eliminate the bias a manager has developed for calling a couple of "go-to" fill-ins by automating a list of who to call and giving the list of candidates a choice in whether or not they want to pick up the extra shift. And, because the process is automated, it is governed by rules that can be explained to employees. While that doesn't mean the employees will always like the rules, they will appreciate that the process can be explained clearly without any surprises.

While technology can be a tremendous enabler for both managers and workers, there are two pitfalls that organizations have to avoid. Avoiding these pitfalls will ensure that the benefits are achieved and will also have a direct impact on employee engagement.

The first pitfall is something we just touched on: transparency. Too often, when new technology is deployed, users are trained on *how* to use the system but not *why* it works the way it does. Therefore, the system is both magical and untrustworthy. Users see the system making complex decisions in the blink of an eye but do not believe the result because they do not understand the logic the system employs. Successful technology rollouts pull the curtain back and explain why the system makes decisions in plain English. Picking up our example, the users simply need to know that the algorithm to fill a shift is based on employee availability, cost, skill, and productivity.

The second pitfall is around the process being automated. Too often, organizations implement new technology and simply try to automate an old, often archaic process. This often increases the cost of the implementation because it requires customization to fit the old process into the new software. It also often makes the system less useable because the user workflow is not naturally built into the system. The best practice is to design a new business process that leverages the important aspects of the existing business process being automated with the workflows the system delivers out of the box.

It's clear that managers need time to develop the relationships with their employees necessary to create engagement. Technology can be used to automate or eliminate low-value administrative tasks, providing managers with more time. But what about the employee? How can technology help increase their engagement?

TECHNOLOGY AS AN EMPLOYEE ENGAGEMENT DRIVER

Employee engagement surveys often ask something like, "Do you have the tools or equipment necessary to perform your job?" Beyond the obvious assessment of whether the person has the materials necessary to perform their job, the question is a good measure of whether employees feel valued, supported, and even empowered at work. For many employees, the answer isn't binary. They may have a tool to help them do their job, but is it a good tool? Does it really help them get the job done, or is it cumbersome, requiring seemingly unnecessary steps? Or is it unreliable? This is further clouded by a relatively new phenomenon called "consumerization."

Consumerization is the shift in enterprise software to adopt principles of consumer software. The smartphone and the Internet have revolutionized the way we think about technology. Employees expect the technology they are given at work to be as simple as the technology they use at home. They expect technology to be simple enough that they don't need instructions to use it. They expect it to be intuitive enough that they can dive deep to perform complex tasks without help and, if they have questions, they rely on the technology or a user community to find the answers. They expect it to be reliable, always on, always updated. When it breaks, they will throw it away and replace it with something that is better.

More and more, the employers that I work with think about technology as a differentiator to attract and retain talent. Simply providing tools is not enough. Providing state-of-the-art technology that enhances the experience at work is the goal. Such technology is being viewed as a force multiplier: it not only enhances the productivity of the tasks, it improves employee engagement that drives even better performance.

There are many technologies that can help engagement, from peer-to-peer recognition platforms to performance management systems. Let's focus on three technologies that have broad applicability and are gaining momentum in enterprise software.

Employee Self-service and Mobile

A couple of years ago, I was preparing to study the impact retail employees at luxury brands had on the customer experience. I was working with a Customer Engagement Management (CEM) provider — one of those companies that conduct the surveys found at the bottom of retail and restaurant receipts. Like most CEM providers, this one also conducted employee engagement surveys, correlating the results to show the relationship between employee engagement and customer engagement.

I was reviewing the questions we had prepared to ask the CEM provider's chief scientist when he said something that astounded me. He said that employers don't understand the impact that they can have by giving employees control of their schedule. He said that time and time again, their employee engagement surveys showed that employees that were given tools to do things like manage their schedules, request time off, or swap shifts with other employees were more engaged than those that didn't. Of course, I have always believed this to be true but have had a hard time finding data to back up that hypothesis. Here was this scientist speaking like it was common knowledge. It was for him, but the rest of the industry hadn't come to terms with it. Now, it has. Aberdeen Group reports that companies that have implemented employee self-service solutions have 18% higher employee engagement stores than those that don't.

Over the last few years, employee self-service adoption has soared among employers. Seventy-four percent of companies have deployed some form of HR employee self-service (Sierra-Cedar, 2014) up from 52% five years ago (CedarCrestone, 2008). And, as adoption increases, the nature of employee self-service is shifting. Early self-service solutions focused on automating low-value transactions such as updating employee information or benefits enrollment. Forms no longer needed to be completed in triplicate — as our cartoon that opens this chapter jibes — because information was captured electronically. This automation certainly benefited both the employer and employee by reducing errors and streamlining processes, but it really didn't impact engagement.

Current self-service solutions are focused on empowering the employee, providing him or her with more autonomy and more control. They provide employees with ready-access to answers and information about the company, compensation, and benefits. They give an employee a say over his or her development path. And, they give employees more control over their work schedules. These are key ingredients to creating employee engagement.

Employee self-service is also being impacted by a shift in technology. Traditionally, employees have accessed self-service through computers at work or via a web browser from home. This limited both manager and employee adoption of self-service for two reasons. First, the computers at work were often inconvenient for employees either by location (e.g. in a break room or other high traffic area) or availability (e.g. a limited number of computers for a large number of employees). Second, due to concerns about overtime and security, hourly and non-exempt employees were often not allowed access to self-service from outside of the corporate firewall. In short, company policies had not kept up with the changing technology. Smartphones have become ubiquitous. Just about every employee has one, and most want to use that device to manage all aspects of their life, including their work life. The mobile phone is a much more convenient channel for most people to check their schedule, pick up an extra shift, or request time off. It creates a great opportunity for employers to increase the adoption and use of self-service features, which, as we have discussed, increases engagement.

Gamification

The second emerging technology impacting employee engagement is gamification. Gamification is the concept of embedding game thinking and game-play elements into non-game applications. It uses points, rewards, badges, and leaderboards to engage users in activities normally not thought of as a game. When used in business, gamification provides employees with recognition and feedback, two important drivers of employee engagement, by rewarding positive behaviors.

Games as a learning tool is not a new idea. Humans have used games to help teach both simple and complex topics for thousands of years. In "The Republic," Plato recounts Socrates saying that people should not be forced to study or forced to train, but rather learn through play. Chess was used in the Middle Ages and Renaissance to teach strategies of war, and video games tied to learning began appearing in the late 1960s and early 1970s. So, it should be no surprise that some of the earliest use of gamification was found in learning management systems.

Ford Motor Company of Canada was an early adopter of this technology, initially introducing gamification to its Learning Management System (LMS). Sales and service employees were rewarded with badges for completing certain tasks or missions that could be displayed in a virtual trophy case. Trivia challenges were issued to help retain and sustain knowledge. Immediately after launch, Ford saw a dramatic increase in site traffic (Bunchball, n.d.). And more people visited the LMS in the first month of the gamification initiative than had done so in the previous year (Lee, 2013). Overall, Ford saw a 417% increase in the use of its LMS and better engagement among its younger audiences (Hein, 2013).

Kronos Incorporated has also introduced gamification to its enterprise workforce management solutions. Individuals and teams are rewarded for accomplishing certain tasks and missions. For example, teams can take the Perfect Payroll Challenge, which rewards employees for things like no missed punches or overtime exceptions. The results of these challenges are displayed on leaderboards, encouraging desired behavior.

Gamification does not need to be limited to pure learning applications or even HR applications. Customer Relationship Management (CRM) systems, the tools used by sales people to track customers and manage sales opportunities, are notoriously risky projects with most analysts suggesting that up to 50% of all CRM implementations do not meet the business's expectations. In an effort to help companies avoid a similar fate, gamification provider Badgeville introduced "Big Game Hunter" for popular CRM provider, Salesforce.com. Salespeople begin the game as "Chicken Hunters" and are rewarded more status for using more and more of the system. According to Badgeville Chief Strategy Officer and Co-Founder Kris Duggan, one customer increased use of the system by 40% (Bradt, 2013).

Analytics

Information overload. I first read that term in Alvin Toffler's seminal 1970 book *Future Shock*, describing an almost dystopian future where people were disconnected, stressed, and disoriented due to rapid changes in a society driven by technology. I did not discover the book until the late-1980s when I found a dog-eared, paperback copy on my dad's bookshelf. Even then — nearly 20 years after the book was first published — the future that Toffler painted seemed very far away.

At the time, I had just gotten my first computer passed down from my grandfather. It was an original IBM PCjr, running MS-DOS with 128 kilobytes of RAM. My computer sported two 5 ¼-inch floppy disk drives that could hold 360 kilobytes of data. All of my college papers and homework assignments for a year could fit easily onto a couple of these floppy disks. (I remember having one disk for each class and thinking it was a luxury.)

Now, 45 years after *Future Shock* was published, the world is producing digital data at an astonishing pace. To understand how much data we're creating and how quickly, we need to talk in zettabytes, which is the same as one trillion gigabytes (or a thousand megabytes, or 3,276 of the 5 ¼-inch floppy disks from my PCjr). In 2009, it was estimated that all of mankind's knowledge required 295 billion gigabytes, or .295 zettabytes, of storage. By 2010, the storage required to hold all data in the world had increased to 1.2 zettabytes. Estimates suggest that these numbers will grow to 7.9 zettabytes of data in 2015 and 35 zettabytes by 2020. The volume stored in enterprise databases are equally staggering. In 2010, .96 zettabytes were stored on corporate database systems. It is expected that this will grow to 6.3 zettabytes in 2015 and 28 zettabytes by 2020 (CSC, 2012). This growth is why Big Data is a big deal! What do we do with all this data?

While organizations are figuring it out by developing Big Data strategies, our employees are suffering from information overload. Data is coming in at such a rapid pace that employees cannot keep up. *The Atlantic* calls this phenomenon "hyperemployment" (Bogost, 2013). Deloitte University Press simply refers to employees as being overwhelmed (Hodson, Schwartz, van Berkel, & Otten, 2014). Frontline employees feel the pinch when customers walk in with their smartphones armed with more and better organized information than the employees have themselves. Patients walk in to hospitals, doctors' offices, and urgent care facilities prepared with a multitude of diagnoses for their symptoms. Shoppers come into stores with more product information than retail associates have immediately available. Users call support desks with troubleshooting steps that customer service representatives have never heard of. Employers need to provide technology to help employees get out from under the weight of this data and start using it to their advantage.

The primary technology employers can provide to their employees is analytics. Analytics is often confused with other data-related technologies. Gartner acknowledges as much in its definition of analytics. Gartner writes, "Analytics has emerged as a catch-all term for a variety of different business intelligence- and application-related initiatives." But, Gartner goes on to say that, "Increasingly, 'analytics' is used to describe statistical and mathematical data analysis that clusters, segments, scores, and predicts what scenarios are most likely to happen." (Gartner, n.d.) Employees need tools that not only report on data, but help them understand and visualize the relationship between disparate pieces of data.

This type of technology can be delivered in two forms. The first is self-service analytics. Employees are given bespoke analytics tools that allow users to access one or more sources of data. That's the benefit of self-service analytics: employees learn one set of analytics tools and can access multiple sources of data. The second delivery mechanism is embedded analytics. As the name implies, embedded analytics are built into other business applications. With embedded analytics, employees see graphs and metrics related to the screens being used. While data is often limited to just the application being viewed, the information is presented in context of the function being used and users do not have to switch from one application to perform an action and another to analyze data related to that action. Both mediums — embedded analytics and self-service analytics — can be delivered through desktops, tablets, or mobile phones.

Analytics can help employees overcome information overload by helping make sense of the massive amounts of information being thrown at them every day. It understands where they need to focus their attention, and it helps them make better decisions faster. All of this creates less stress and helps employees feel more in control of their work.

CONCLUSION

Smart employers recognize that technology can help improve employee engagement in a number of ways. Managers can use technology to automate activities giving them more time to spend with employees, a critical factor in driving employee engagement. Emerging technology such as employee self-service, gamification, mobile enhancements, or analytics help employees perform their day-to-day work in a more efficient and enjoyable manner. Employers who choose not to provide employees with technologies that make their work lives better run the risk of losing those employees and the value they bring to the bottom line.

With the Spring semester coming to an end, the beautiful weather wasn't the only thing keeping a smile on Bobbie's face. "I found a great summer program for Nicole, and with just one summer class, I updated my availability in our new system so my work schedule is  perfect! I can even pick up extra shifts with my phone!" The new system at Bobbie's work allows employees to update their personal and benefits information, request shifts to work, request vacation time, and even track their training. "It's a cool system," says Bobbie. "I can easily take care of quick work stuff on my phone or even on my school iPad, but what I LOVE is how I get points for easy stuff like just showing up and being on time. We also can get points for high training scores. Of all the employees, I'm first in points — and my brother isn't too happy about it!"

REFERENCES

Bogost, I. (2013, November 8). *Hyperemployment, or the Exhausting Work of the Technology User.* Retrieved from The Atlantic: http://www.theatlantic.com/technology/archive/2013/11/hyperemployment-or-the-exhausting-work-of-the-technology-user/281149/

Bradt, G. (2013, July 3). *How Salesforce And Deloitte Tackle Employee Engagement With Gamification.* Retrieved from Forbes: http://www.forbes.com/sites/george-bradt/2013/07/03/how-salesforce-and-deloitte-tackle-employee-engagement-with-gamification/

Bunchball. (n.d.). *How Ford Motor Company of Canada shifted sales, parts and service teams into high gear.* Retrieved from Bunchball: http://www.bunchball.com/customers/ford

CedarCrestone. (2008). *CedarCrestone 2008-2009 HR Systems Survey, 11th Annual Edition.* Alpharetta: CedarCrestone. Retrieved from http://www.sierra-cedar.com/wp-content/uploads/sites/12/2014/07/CedarCrestone_2008-2009_HRSS_WP.pdf

CSC. (2012). *Big Data Universe Beginning to Explode.* Retrieved from CSC: http://www.csc.com/insights/flxwd/78931-big_data_universe_beginning_to_explode

De Smet, A., McGurk, M., & Vinson, M. (2009). Unlocking the Potential of Frontline Managers. *McKinsey Quarterly.* Retrieved from http://www.mckinsey.com/insights/organization/unlocking_the_potential_of_frontline_managers/

Gartner. (n.d.). *Gartner IT Glossary > Analytics.* Retrieved from Gartner: http://www.gartner.com/it-glossary/analytics

Harder, J. K., Schmidt, F. L., Argawal, S., & Plowman, S. K. (2013, February). *The Relationship between Employee Engagement and Orga nizational Outcomes.* Retrieved from Gallup: http://www.gallup.com/services/177047/q12-meta-analysis.aspx

Hein, R. (2013, June 06). *How to Use Gamification to Engage Employees.* Retrieved from CIO: http://www.cio.com/article/2453330/careers-staffing/how-to-use-gamification-to-engage-employees.html

Hodson, T., Schwartz, J., van Berkel, A., & Otten, I. W. (2014, March 7). *The Overwhelmed Employee.* Retrieved from Deloitte University Press: http://dupress.com/articles/hc-trends-2014-overwhelmed-employee/

Kaufman, J., Markey, R., Burton, S. D., & Azzarello, D. (2013). *Who's Responsible for Employee Engagement.* Stockholm: Netsurvey. Retrieved from Netsurvey.

Lee, J. (2013, April 08). *The Three F's of Successful Gamifcation.* Retrieved from Retail TouchPoints: http://www.retailtouchpoints.com/retail-crm/2440-the-three-fs-of-successful-gamification

Sierra-Cedar. (2014). *Sierra-Cedar 2014 – 2015 HR Systems Survey White Paper, 17th Annual Edition.* Alpharetta: Sierra-Cedar. Retrieved from http://www.sierra-cedar.com/wp-content/uploads/sites/12/2014/11/Sierra-Cedar_2014-2015_HRSys-temsSurveyWhitepaper.pdf

Section 2

PUT THE BEST TEAM ON THE FIELD

Bob's first day on the job was eye-opening. As the new Director of Professional Services, he had an office, but all he could hear from it were the sobs of the Vice President's admin in a nearby cube. Walking the rows of cubes, Bob observed heads down quiet. Right at 5:00, an informal parade of individuals made their way out of the building. At least the sobbing had stopped. That night, Bob told his wife he may have made a mistake taking the new job, even though the compensation was way better than what he had left. Bob's wife asked, "So what are you going to do about it?" The next day just before lunch, Bob popped his head into the cubes of his employees, some peers, and his boss's admin and said, "Hey, let's have lunch in the café." It went well. Everyone received nutrition. Stories were told. Some laughed — mostly Bob. His laugh was infectious. Nobody cried.

CHAPTER THREE

Culture Drives Results

David Almeda

Chief People Officer, Kronos Incorporated

Corporate culture is sometimes viewed as an intangible aspect of an organization, set apart from "tangibles" like sales, revenue, and profitability. But the truth is that corporate culture is a critical component of any successful organization, and every organization has a culture, whether it is purposefully designed and managed or not. An organization's culture impacts how employees relate to one another, how they interact with managers and how they service customers. In short, corporate culture has a direct impact on employee engagement and the bottom line.

In 1992, Harvard Business School professors James L. Heskett and John P. Kotter published a fascinating and influential book on the topic of corporate culture and how it drives financial results. In *Corporate Culture and Performance*, the authors exhaustively researched 207 companies within 22 industries between 1977 and 1988, arguing that strong corporate cultures that facilitate adaptation to a changing world are associated with strong financial results. Their research indicated that corporate cultures that highly value employees, customers, and owners while encouraging leadership from everyone in the firm do better financially.

One exhibit[1] from the book highlights the difference in results over an 11-year period between 12 companies that had performance-enhancing cultures and 20 companies that did not:

The results are eye opening and as good an argument as any for what may seem like common sense: organizations with cultures designed to help employees succeed do better.

Average Increase for 12 Firms with Performance-Enhancing Cultures	Average Increase for 20 Firms without Performance-Enhancing Cultures
Revenue Growth 682%	Revenue Growth 166%
Employment Growth 282%	Employment Growth 36%
Stock Price Growth 901%	Stock Price Growth 74%
Net Income Growth 756%	Net Income Growth 1%

So how can your organization design and manage a corporate culture that will help drive success?

Step 1: Understand the Current Culture

As previously stated, every company has a culture whether it is purposefully designed and managed or not. If you think your company does not have a culture, you just don't know what it is. Before you can design the corporate culture you want, you must first take steps to understand the one you have.

So how do you do this?

There are a variety of ways that organizations can get a handle on the current state of their corporate culture. One important method is surveying one's own employee population. Administering and analyzing engagement surveys enables an organization to hear from its own employees about how they experience and perceive the corporate culture. How do employees feel about their work environment, the leadership team, and the formal and informal interactions they have with peers? Do they feel there are ample opportunities for learning and development? Are rewards and recognition programs motivating the right behaviors? As outlined in Bob Clements' chapter, do employees have access to resources and tools that enable them to do their jobs effectively? The only way you will know the answers to these questions is to ask.

It can also be valuable, in many instances, to work with a third party vendor to review benchmarking data in your industry. How do you stack up when it comes to employee satisfaction? How about compensation and benefits? In today's social society with outlets like Glassdoor and LinkedIn, the state of corporate culture has never been more transparent. You need to know what else is out there because, undoubtedly, your employees already do. There is great value in gaining a realistic perspective on how your organization is the same, different, better, and/or worse than others in your field.

Don't forget that it is very likely you are already collecting data via your Human Resource Information System (HRIS) that you could use to flesh out the picture of what your corporate culture really looks like. Analyzing at both a micro and macro level the nuts-and-bolts data, like age and experience range of new hires, tenure, and turnover, can provide you with insight into who your employees are and what they want.

Along with robust quantitative data, you also want to leverage qualitative data. Run focus groups with employees to hear about what they like and don't like about how they work with peers, interact with managers and executives, and complete their jobs on a daily basis. Do they understand the design of the organization? Are they aware of the vision and values important to the company? Hearing anecdotes from employees about both their good and bad experiences at work can inform your view of your company's strengths, weaknesses, and opportunities.

Remember to look beyond just employees in gathering qualitative data. Check in with customers as well about how they perceive your organization. Do they like doing business with you? How do they perceive your culture? How do they think you treat employees? Are they getting exceptional service or is that not something they associate with your organization? Soliciting the opinions of your customers on these topics, both informally and formally, provides you with an alternative point-of-view and also lets your customers know that you value their thoughts and perspective.

A key to making this information-gathering process as valuable as possible is ensuring that this analysis be done at multiple organizational levels so that perspective-specific bias doesn't leak into the results. Taking a deep-dive into these areas will help you clearly define what your current culture is.

Step 2: Define the Target Culture
Now that you have put in the work to understand the culture you have, it's time to start thinking about the culture you want. Think about your current culture and determine what attributes need to be added to it in order for the organization to successfully meet its strategic objectives.

It may help to think of this process as an exercise in constructing a structure with building blocks. In most cases, the current culture will have a number of attributes that have been valuable in getting the organization to where it is today. Think of these attributes as your solid foundation: you want to keep them and build upon them. Modifying the culture requires that new attributes, or blocks, be added to the existing base. You are not looking to knock down everything that has been built just for the sake of having a fresh start. It's about taking what you already do well and adding to it.

It's also critical to focus on building new areas of strength, rather than just discontinuing bad habits. You need to think in terms of "What do we need to start doing?" not "What do we need to stop?" A parent may think of it the way they do when dealing with their children. In my experience, telling my kids to stop doing something is, generally speaking, ineffective. For example, "Stop throwing your coat on the floor when you get home," tends to result in little change. What does work with my kids is telling them what to start doing and thus, "Hang up your coat on this hook when you get home," has been proven, at least in my small and admittedly unscientific sample study, to get better results. The same approach holds true with organizations. Give employees clear direction on how you want them to behave towards one another and towards customers and you'll be working with them to create the corporate culture you want.

Step 3: Use the Tools at Your Disposal to Shape the Culture

The diagram on the next page, courtesy of The Boston Consulting Group (BCG), provides a useful framework for talking about the factors in an organization that impact culture.

Leadership, people and development, rewards and recognition, informal interactions, organizational design, resources and tools, vision and values, and the work environment itself are all absolutely critical factors that contribute to corporate culture. They can also, in one way or another, be viewed as levers that can be pulled to encourage various outcomes.

Organizations need to think carefully about which levers can be pulled to align the current culture with the target one. For example, if a key tenet

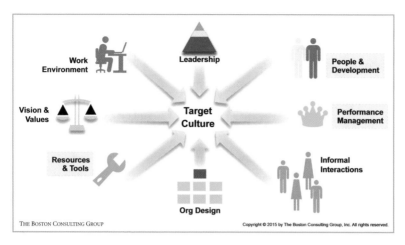

of your corporate culture is providing exceptional customer service, make sure that employees who do this are rewarded with spot bonuses or formal recognition programs. If respecting co-workers is a critical part of your corporate DNA, make sure it is something that employees are measured on. If having fun is central to your mission, make sure your leadership team is not a dour bunch of bean counters.

I had the privilege of seeing a very successful lever pulling endeavor in my role as Vice President of Human Resources at Staples Inc., one of the country's leading office supply stores, in the early 2000s. The company's tagline at the time was, "That was easy." Expanding on that theme, 2005 ads featured a large red push-button marked "easy." Following a television campaign featuring the "Easy Button," it was turned into a real product that was shipped to stores in the U.S., Canada, and Germany starting in the fall of 2005. The buttons really took off, and the whole campaign was widely considered a great branding success.

What customers may not realize, however, was that prior to launching this well-known campaign, Staples put plans in place to ensure that the store experience was aligned with the marketing. Promising "easy" and delivering "hard" would have been a public relations and sales disaster. To avoid this, as part of their pre-launch efforts, Staples changed their store employee incentive plans. The company identified the four or five employee behaviors that drove customer satisfaction, and incented stores and store employees that exhibited those behaviors. Similar to how process changes at Tesco led to increased sales as described by Mark Wales in Chapter 1, customer satisfaction increased which in turn drove meaningful same-store sales increases across the chain, and backed up the "easy" messaging.

While this is a great "lever pulling" success story, organizations must be aware that making changes to any of these aspects of company life — pulling levers — can have unintended consequences. For example, changing incentive compensation to reward Outcome A comes at the expense of the current outcomes that are being incentivized. Likewise, changing your organization's vision and values too frequently can make them appear temporary, subject to change, and therefore less important to pay attention to. Organizations need to consider these unintended consequences when designing the culture, and not oversimplify things by focusing only on the potential positive cultural impact of change.

Step 4: Plan the Change

Academically speaking, it would be interesting to see what would happen in an organization if multiple change levers were pulled at the same time. Practically, such action has the potential to create a nightmare scenario. This is why most organizations take a phased approach to changing culture.

To use another example from my work at Staples, when the company wanted to create a culture that would make it "easy" for customers to buy products in their stores, they took a multi-pronged approach to cultural change. Phase One focused on improving the work environment as well as on improving systems and tools. Store layouts were modified to make it easier to find products. Procedures were revised to eliminate long check-out lines and unnecessary interactions with cashiers. Inventory procedures and technology were updated to increase inventory levels so that the items that customers were most frequently looking for were available.

Phase Two focused on people and development as well as rewards and recognition. All store employees were trained to consistently demonstrate the customer-facing behaviors that Staples knew would make it easier for customers. For instance, employees were encouraged to walk customers to the product they were seeking as opposed to telling them where the product was located in the store. To reinforce these behaviors, as described earlier in the chapter, Staples implemented a team incentive program for all employees that rewarded store teams based on reaching specific customer satisfaction goals. In the end, the approach that Staples took was effective because they pulled the correct cultural change levers, in the right sequence, at the right time.

In general, organizations should think about implementing material cultural modifications over a one- to two-year period of time. This approach enables employers to understand what the impact of one set of changes is prior to moving on to the next. Organizations also have a finite ability to absorb change. Move too fast and culture modification becomes a box-checking exercise that will not have the intended or needed impact on culture.

Step 5: Calibrate

Culture is a fluid and ever-changing entity. What works in one quarter/year/decade may fail miserably in the next. Compounding the complexity, Human Resources functions have been notoriously slow to adopt the kind of talent analytics that can help with their culture-related calibration efforts.

According to HR analyst firm Bersin by Deloitte, most companies spend about one-half to two-thirds of all of their expenses on people. Despite the big price tag, most organizations do not invest the necessary time or money to truly understand and unlock the value of their people data to help make better labor-related decisions.[2]

Whether it's that organizations lack the money to capture and analyze people data, or that they lack the analytical competency to see the value in and execute such work, the absence of data-driven analysis of people-related issues is a material barrier to constructing an optimal corporate culture. Cultural modification is not for the faint of heart. Attempting to modify a culture without accurate data is like trying to cross the open sea, blind-folded and without any type of navigation device. You might get where you need to go eventually, but few would volunteer to climb aboard for that type of journey.

Optimal success in this area requires that companies employ measurement tools — those same surveys, third party engagements, and focus groups we talked about using to understand one's own culture — to ensure that cultural modification efforts are having the intended impact. To this mix, employers should also look at adding downstream Key Performance Indicators (KPIs) such as talent retention, applicant flow, and productivity measures to obtain a more informed view of the impact of their culture modification related efforts. A robust, multi-faceted view allows organizations to make better decisions. Simply put, it allows an organization to more deeply understand if their efforts to date have been effective. If the answer is yes, an organization should stay the course. If the answer is no, it's time to return to Step 3 and see what other levers might be pulled to bring the current culture closer to the target.

PUTTING IT ALL TOGETHER

Understanding your current culture, defining your target culture, using the tools at your disposal to shape the culture, planning for change, and calibrating results are critical steps in creating a successful corporate culture. But these steps alone won't guarantee success.

According to Heskett and Kotter, successful organizations with adaptive cultures share another important trait: "Excellent leadership from the top seems to be the essential ingredient…. This leadership empowers other managers and employees who see the need for change but have been constrained by the old culture. It also helps win over the hearts and minds of others who have not yet recognized the necessity of major change."[3]

In the end, flexibility and acceptance of change need to be components of any successful culture. It sounds simple, but is actually incredibly hard to do. Building a strong organization is all about establishing a culture of trust, transparency, and ongoing communication with employees. Change is inevitable, but if employees understand why the changes are being made, are confident that you are telling them the truth, and trust that you have their best interests at heart, change will not negatively impact culture or employee engagement. If the above conditions are not met, change can magnify existing cultural deficiencies and create new ones.

Equally important, organizations that have leaders who consistently demonstrate a sincere interest in their employees' professional and personal well-being, regularly communicate in a way that marries employees' daily work to the larger company strategy, and understand the impact of their leadership shadow on the organization are the ones well on their way to having a corporate culture that truly drives results.

A year after Bob's first lunch meeting, the culture within his group had certainly changed — and other departments were taking notice. Bob had found a willing partner in his organization's HR leader and change efforts in his department had been serving as a pilot program  for how culture change could be driven across the organization. Employees' feedback was being solicited, they felt they were being heard, and many of their recommendations for improving the business were being reviewed by the senior team. People were hanging out in each other's offices, cross-functional projects were advancing, and the business results were tracking better than ever. The crying had stopped. The laughter hadn't. Bob and his team were energized and kept coming up with great ideas to push the business forward.

ENDNOTES

1   John P. Kotter, James L. Heskett, *Corporate Culture and Performance*, (New York: The Free Press, 1992), p.78.

2   Josh Bersin, "Predictions for 2015: Redesigning the Organization for a Rapidly Changing World," Deloitte Development LLC, January 2015.

3   John P. Kotter, James L. Heskett, *Corporate Culture and Performance*, (New York: The Free Press, 1992), p.150.

Bob rolled his eyes when his boss suggested that he hire the Millennial candidate for the Marketing Manager position he was looking to fill. A Baby Boomer, Bob wanted to hire the Gen-Xer with more experience and a more "traditional" view on what work is. "I'm concerned Brittany will be a problem — between her desire to work remotely and all her questions about our social media policy," lamented Bob. Elaine, Bob's boss, smiled. "Bob, Brittany is a very bright candidate, and does it really matter where she works if she gets the job done? Are you less productive when you work from home to watch your grand-daughter?" "What about the Twitting?" Bob questioned. Elaine's smile broadened. "Bob, social media is part of who they are. I'm on Facebook and Twitter, too. And maybe Brittany will Tweet about what a great experience she's having here." Bob begrudgingly asked his HR Business partner to extend the offer to Brittany.

CHAPTER FOUR

How to Best Attract and Retain Millennials

Dan Schawbel

Managing Partner, Millennial Branding, LLC

Founder, WorkplaceTrends.com

2015 marked the year that Millennials became the highest percentage of the U.S. workforce. They have various qualities that make them different than Generation Xers and Baby Boomers. Companies are having trouble understanding the needs of Millennial candidates and engaging them in a way which is authentic and encouraging. As a result, Millennials only stay at a company for two years on average before jumping to a new position at a different company. This is a major issue for companies who are looking to drive performance and fill their leadership gaps.

As 10,000 Baby Boomers retire on a daily basis, and more Millennials job hop, companies are going to suffer. Not only are companies under pressure to create retention programs for Millennials, but they will also have to compete for the top Millennial candidates. As more Millennials either flock to companies that have "Millennial-friendly" work environments, or start their own businesses, many companies will have trouble innovating and remaining competitive. Companies need to engage with students even before they graduate if they want to be in a graduate's selection criteria. Organizations that start building relationships with students earlier on, and create an appealing culture, will have a competitive advantage now and in the future.

WHO ARE MILLENNIALS AND HOW ARE THEY DIFFERENT?

Millennials are misunderstood and the media propagates all of their flaws on a daily basis. As a Millennial myself, and someone who has studied my generation through nearly two dozen research studies, my goal is to paint a true picture for you. First, Millennials are 80 million strong in the United States, which is four million more than the Boomer generation. We were born between 1982 and 1993 and we are extremely tech savvy, globally connected, optimistic, and collaborative. Other terms for Millennials include Generation Y and the digital natives.

Through our research with American Express, we've found that Generation X and Baby Boomers view Millennials as entitled, having poor work ethic, being easily distracted, self-centered, and disloyal. These are the common criticisms and stereotypes that Millennials have had to deal with since entering the workforce. Through another study we did with Randstad, we found that Millennials stereotype Generation Z, the generation that comes after Millennials and who started entering the workforce around 2015, as being lazy. While every generation has a negative view of the upcoming generation, they also have a positive view of their elders. For instance, Generation Z views Millennials as being open-minded, having new ideas, and being creative, while Millennials view Generation X and Boomers as being wise and willing to mentor.

Millennials might have been entitled years ago when their workplace expectations were too high and misaligned, but no more. The economy has delayed their adulthood and many are still living with their parents or siblings in order to save money and because they can't afford high rents. They are getting married later, having children later, and are struggling to pay back student loans. A study by Bentley University, my alma mater, found that 84% of Millennials say that helping to make a positive difference in the world is more important than professional recognition, and a separate study by Telefonica found that about half believe that a decent paying job is a privilege. Another common Millennial stereotype is that Millennials are narcissistic, yet all generations are posting about their lives online daily and taking "selfies." Millennials just grew up with it.

While many companies believe they can attract Millennials to work at their company because they have a pool table or free beer, that isn't the case. Millennials are looking for meaningful work and to make a positive difference in the world. They want to have time to be with their family and friends and are less likely to work at companies that infringe on their personal time. That's why you see more Millennials choosing employers that provide flexible work options that allow them to balance their work and private lives.

Compared to Millennials, Generation X has 45 million people who were born between 1965 and 1981, and Baby Boomers have 76 million people who were born between 1945 and 1964. Generation X is known to be skeptical, stressed out, and seeking work-life balance. Baby Boomers, on the other hand, believe in working for one company for a longer period of time, and that status should be based on how many years you've worked at a company. While Millennials believe in continuous learning, Generation X feels that training creates loyalty and Baby Boomers think that if you train employees, they will leave. When it comes to education, Millennials view it as an expense, whereas Generation X views it as a way to get to the next level in their careers, and Baby Boomers think it is part of their birthright.

HOW COMPANIES CAN BEST RECRUIT
AND RETAIN MILLENNIALS

When I talk to companies on a daily basis, they aren't complaining about recruiting Millennials as much as they are about retaining them. We've done numerous studies that point to Millennials only staying with a company for two years before moving on. If you compare that to older generations, Generation X stays five years and Baby Boomers stay seven years before leaving for a new company.

There are many reasons why Millennials leave your company.

First, since their adulthood has been delayed, many Millennials didn't have the time or opportunity to learn more about themselves and the type of company culture and work they wanted to focus on post-graduation. They take a job at a company and soon realize that it isn't a good fit for them in the first place. This is why the best retention strategy is a strong recruiting strategy. If you hire for cultural fit, it increases the chances that an employee will stay with you longer. The second reason is because talent is much more accessible today than in the past decade. Through services like LinkedIn, the best Millennial talent is being bombarded with new job offers and Millennials are willing to switch for a better culture and/or more money. This puts more pressure on companies to create a unique culture that supports Millennials and gives them competitive benefits and salaries. Third, if managers are really bad at setting expectations for their employees and if Millennials don't see opportunities to move up, they move out. Your job is to set honest expectations for younger workers so they know that if they stay longer, they will be rewarded with a better title, more money, and opportunities to grow.

These retention issues cost companies a lot of money, especially those with hundreds or thousands of Millennial employees. A few years ago, we did a study and found that it costs $20,000 to replace each Millennial employee. If you lose one hundred employees, that's $2 million. What's worse is that by losing employees, it puts more pressure on other workers to fill in and it can take months to replace each worker. In the same Randstad study previously mentioned, we found that Millennials want to work with subject matter experts who have a great work ethic. By hiring talented Millennials, you will naturally attract more talented Millennials, so use your talent as a recruiting tool. Furthermore, identify key traits of candidates to ensure they are willing to work hard and inspire their co-workers to do the same.

One way to ensure that Millennials stay at your company is to give them a higher purpose. A recent Deloitte study found that Millennials want to work for a company that is making a difference in society, not just a profit for shareholders. We've found that over a third of Millennials want their employer to give back to the community. At Microsoft, 65% of employees raise money for various charities by participating in more than 300 activities including a 5k run and an online auction. At JetBlue, 1,900 crewmembers and volunteers have donated their time to plant more than 1,200 trees. Ernst & Young has "EY Connect Day," a day of service that has enabled employees to log more than 60,000 hours of service annually. Each of these companies not only creates volunteer programs, but also communicates them to their employees and the public at large. They do this to show that they aren't just in business to make money but actually care about making a difference. This engages Millennials on a deeper level. In order to connect with Millennials, managers must show them how the projects they work on benefit the team, the company, the customers, and the world. When you hire Millennials, you want to project your vision, mission, and values because they must be aligned to retain them.

Another important benefit that employees are looking for when deciding who to work for is work flexibility. The demands of the workplace are constantly increasing, and we've moved from a 40-hour workweek to a 49-hour workweek. In America at least, everyone is always working, yet Millennials want time to spend on personal activities. They don't believe in the nine-to-five workday and want to integrate their personal and professional lives together. Technology has enabled them to work from home, while still collaborating. There are fewer barriers between what they do in the office and what they do at home. A recent study we conducted with the CareerArc group found that 30% of employers expect employees to be accessible outside of the office by phone and email. Due to the growing demand of Millennials wanting a more flexible workplace, more companies are creating programs that allow them to work remotely on a regular basis. For instance, at Aetna, about half of employees work from home full-time. It's saved the company tens of millions of dollars in real-estate-related costs as a result.

Another great way to engage Millennials is to invest in their careers through training and development. Millennials want to learn as much as they can because they are still early in their careers. Create mentoring programs to pair them up with executives. Let them teach your executives how to use new technology for their benefit and then have your executives support their career aspirations. This way, Millennials will feel more connected at your company, work harder, and have support when their manager isn't around. Aside from mentoring, Millennials also seek real-time feedback, enjoy learning from gamified applications, and often choose to enroll in both rotational and leadership development programs.

Real-time feedback helps Millennials improve along the way rather than have to wait a year to see what they did right and wrong. Adobe substituted their annual performance reviews for a continuous check-in approach and has increased their retention rate as a result.

Gamification, as Bob Clements and Sharlyn Lauby discussed in depth in their chapters, is becoming a hot topic, and Millennials are the driving force because they grew up playing video games and that's how they learned and developed as people. By using applications you can create simulations that allow them to perform actions without actually performing them. Additionally, gamified applications create competition between Millennials, forcing them to learn and constantly improve so they can keep up with their peers.

Rotational programs have always appealed to Millennials, who use them to figure out what they want to do with their careers, while traveling and experiencing different departments. Many organizations complain that their investment in these programs doesn't pay off because Millennials end up leaving anyway. In order to prevent that, companies need to create a better transition period between the program and the full-time job. They also need to do a better job of pairing the Millennial employee's strengths and personality with the right job and group.

One of the biggest complaints from Millennials is that there aren't enough opportunities to move up in an organization. Part of why that happens is because companies insist on hiring more externally than from within. It costs about 1.7 times as much to hire externally since you have to advertise for the job, pay a staffing firm, and then there are the productivity losses from having a void on a team. By hiring internally, you are giving Millennials a chance to grow and move either vertically or horizontally through your corporation. Hiring internally allows your talent to develop, increases employee morale, saves you money, and it takes weeks to hire someone internally versus months for external hires.

When I speak about Millennials, I have no choice but to talk about their use of technology. It's not only what audiences and customers want to hear, but technology is one of the three biggest movements that have influenced Millennial behaviors (family and the economy are the other two). A recent Jobvite survey reports that 94% of companies use social media to recruit, and more and more job seekers are using their smartphones to find work. What's even more interesting than using technology to recruit is using it to connect Millennials in the workplace. When I worked at EMC, we created "EMC ONE," an online community where employees could blog, create wikis, and share documents. Before I left EMC, we had about a fourth of all employees using EMC ONE. It was powerful because it flattened the organization, created stronger networks, and helped people solve problems faster. In order to appeal to Millennials, companies need to embrace technology from the top down, use internal social networks to engage them, and never block social media sites.

Aside from technology, Millennials have been inspired by entrepreneurship. Now that the cost of building a business is much cheaper, and information on how to build a business is free on the Internet, Millennials view entrepreneurship as an alternative to a "real job." Companies can attract these entrepreneurial Millennials by providing internal support systems and resources that allow them to act like a startup founder while in a company. For instance, LinkedIn has their [in]cubator program where employees collaborate on an idea and then pitch it to executives. If it gets funded, the team will work on the project, which will potentially have a high ROI for the company. Google has the 20% program where employees spend 20% of their time doing projects outside of their job description. These are only two examples but they both empower Millennials to use the resources — and brand — of a larger company to pursue their entrepreneurial ambitions.

Our research also shows that Millennials want honest leadership. They desperately want business leaders to be transparent and to be included in more discussions. Millennials are the first generation to actively talk about their salaries in the workplace, something that most companies try to discourage as it can end up costing them money and potentially creating a hostile environment due to perceived or real inequality. The reality is that Millennials don't trust Chief Executive Officers, politicians, or any other business leaders, so your job, as an organization, is to gain their trust. The more you are upfront about your workplace expectations and the health of your company, the more your younger workers will trust you and work harder for you. If you aren't honest with them, they will find out anyway by Googling or asking other employees.

Of course different workers have different needs and desires. There are several strategies that can help retain younger workers — offering flexibility, training and development, real-time feedback, rotational programs and growth potential, technology and social collaboration, entrepreneurship opportunities, and honest leadership — which all can be used to show how Millennials connect to a higher purpose within the organization.

DON'T FORGET ABOUT GENERATION Z

I've spoken a lot about Millennials, but we also need to look ahead to the upcoming generation, Generation Z. Millennials have graduated college, or are at the age that they could have graduated college. Generation Z is going to college or entering the workplace at a time when there are approximately 50 million job openings in America but not enough talent to fill those positions. It's a time when America lacks skilled labor in a variety of industries such as healthcare, engineering, accounting, and the skilled trades. I disagree when people say "there aren't enough jobs" or "there's too much competition for jobs." The fact is that Generation Zers are applying for jobs where there's high demand and short supply. The magic bullet to getting a job is to focus on areas with the most supply and the least competition. Companies who have gaps in their talent pool need to invest in the next generation in order to close their skills gap.

In order to close their skills gap, organizations need to get closer to colleges and other sources of supply for skilled workers. Based on our research, colleges aren't doing the best job preparing students for the real world. Most classes are still the same, using the same text books, taught by the same teachers, many of whom don't have real world experience. Companies should start sponsoring classes, having some of their workers teach at schools they recruit from, and telling schools exactly where the demand is. College presidents and heads of HR should meet in person to discuss the types of skills and curriculum that will help fill skills gaps. When companies offer internships, we've found that many of those internships don't convert into jobs later. Companies that invest in interns should be trying harder to fill their open full-time positions with these interns.

Another thing that needs to change is timing: when companies target students and when students should start targeting companies. Currently, career service centers at colleges tell students that they should wait until their junior year to get an internship. This is bad advice because the best way to get an internship is to already have an internship. I know because I graduated with eight of them. Companies should try to recruit freshman and sophomores and then maintain that talent through multiple internships until they finally get hired for full-time jobs. Companies should also have some of their employees guest lecture and go to career events in order to build their brand and showcase why their industry is so appealing. Career centers should push students to start applying to companies during their freshman year to best prepare them for the road ahead.

The way in which you engage with students is important, too. First, you want to have a presence at the career fairs of schools that you regularly recruit at. Second, you want to have a social media presence that showcases why you're the best place to work for a specific type of student. You can use pictures of your office, stories from your employees, video interviews, and more to allow students to see what you're all about. Third, you want to engage students in and outside of the classroom. You can do this by having your employees participate in school events such as conferences, networking events, meet and greets, mock interviews, and more. Finally, you can use games that allow students to get to know your company better. For instance, Marriott has a game on their Facebook page where you can become a chef and learn what it takes to be a successful one.

Millennials are quickly becoming the most influential generation in the workforce so companies have to pay attention to them. They aren't just looking for a paycheck and want to align themselves with companies that are making a positive impact on the world. Companies have to support their interests, train them, and give them internal opportunities so they can succeed.

Twenty months later, Brittany is a star performer on Bob's team. Her marketing programs are fresh, creative, and have built more pipeline than those of her more experienced peers. She learned the business at a furious rate, and improved everyone's performance by introducing

gamification techniques and training the team on how to amplify their messages with social media. Brittany even made time to volunteer on the company charitable giving committee. Bob is genuinely impressed by Brittany's performance, and personally moved by her devotion to giving back. "If Millennials are selfish," Bob thought, "She's an exception." During her annual performance appraisal, Bob rated Brittany a 3.5 — right between "Good" and "Very Good." In Bob's mind, Brittany still has a lot to learn, but he did get her a little extra bump in pay. He wanted Brittany to know her work was appreciated.

Brittany came into the office for her weekly one-on-one with Bob, and right away he sensed something wasn't right. "What's up? You OK?" Bob asked. "Bob, I'm frustrated! There's one goal I still haven't been able to achieve." "How can I help?" asked Bob. Brittany smiled and said, "You can let me teach you how to use Twitter."

It was the lunch rush and Bobbie was so busy taking customer
orders that she almost stopped worrying about Ronnie, the
youngest of her three children, a kindergartner. Ronnie was
listless at breakfast, and Bobbie was worried he might be
coming down with something. With a heating oil delivery on
the way and the holidays coming up, Bobbie couldn't afford to
miss any work. Her supervisor was very understanding, but the
restaurant didn't offer workers paid time off, so a missed day
meant no pay. During her shift, Bobbie's regular customers
chatted her up and brought a smile to her face, but she couldn't
get Ronnie out of her mind. Between refilling coffee and wiping
down tables, she resolved to head home that night and spend
time looking for a job that offered at least some sick days.

CHAPTER FIVE

Just Because You Can, Doesn't Mean You Should

Susan R. Meisinger, SPHR, JD

Columnist, Speaker, Consultant

Former President and Chief Executive Officer, Society for Human

Resource Management (SHRM)

Before I was Chief Executive Officer of the Society for Human Resource Management (SHRM) I worked for the U.S. Department of Labor, where I led an agency that enforced a number of federal labor laws. I was responsible for enforcement of the federal minimum wage, overtime, and child labor laws, as well as the non-discrimination and affirmative action obligations for federal contractors, to name a few. In all, I was charged with enforcement or administration of more than 90 federal laws with a little more than 4,000 employees.

During my years at the Department, I saw the good, the bad, and the ugly in how employers treat their workers. And I came away with a firmly held view that the vast majority of employers just want to do the right thing by their employees. They want to abide by all of the employment laws — if someone would just please explain to them how to do it, and if the government would just make the laws and regulations easily understandable.

I also came to realize that laws are drafted to address the lowest common denominator of employer behavior. Frequently, legislation is enacted in response to a story about how workers were mistreated by their employer. The mistreatment makes the evening news, and members of the legislature — federal or state — decide to investigate and hold hearings to learn more. Frequently, the result is legislation to make sure the mistreatment stops, with regulation of some aspect of employers' employment practices.

Sometimes the legislation is the result of widespread bad practices of employers — such as the poor safety standards more than a hundred years ago that led to the Triangle Shirt Factory fire disaster.[1] A fire spread rapidly through a cramped garment factory in New York City, killing 146 workers. The building had only one fire escape, which collapsed and workers were crushed as they struggled with doors that were locked by managers to prevent theft. The disaster led to new workplace safety standards in the State of New York, which set an example for the rest of the country.

Sometimes, it's a practice that a relatively few employers adopt, but which insults the sensibilities of the public and legislature, which in turn leads to legislation to ensure that no more employers adopt the practice. For me, requiring applicants to disclose social media usernames and passwords is such a practice. While a few employers believe that access to personal accounts is needed, most, including me, consider requiring such access to be an invasion of a candidate's privacy. States have agreed, and as of 2015, 19 states have enacted legislation that makes such demands illegal, and such legislation has been introduced or considered in at least 23 states.[2]

Whatever the reason for the regulation, the result is a legal compliance landscape that sometimes feels like a minefield. With hundreds of federal and state labor laws already enacted, and more being considered every day, human resource executives are forced to spend a great deal of time, energy, and money trying to ensure that their company is in full compliance.

Often, an employer's decision on what employment practices to adopt are based on the easiest path: they simply adopt employment policies that mirror the minimum requirements set out in law. If the federal Fair Labor Standards Act requires overtime pay after 40 hours of work, then overtime is only paid after 40 hours of work. If the federal Family and Medical Leave Act requires unpaid leave for 12 weeks, then unpaid leave is provided, and for just 12 weeks.

But what may seem like a good business decision — to provide exactly what the law requires — because it's safe and you believe it will be easy to administer and put the business on an equal footing with competitors, may not be such a great idea.

While employment practices have to be considered and adopted to best meet the needs of each individual business, sometimes the path of simply following the law overlooks the competitive advantage that may be gained by going above and beyond the law. Sometimes, what may seem more costly and complicated is really more competitive and profitable.

MINIMUM WAGE

As of July 2009, the federal minimum wage was set at $7.25 per hour. Effective January 2015, 29 states have a minimum wage higher than the federal minimum, some established because of automatic adjustments, others through legislation or ballot initiatives.[3]

Many unskilled jobs are typically "minimum wage jobs." Since employers can find people who are willing to work for minimum wage, that's what many employers pay. These employers frequently argue that they have to keep their labor costs as low as possible to be competitive with other businesses.

But should you recommend that your company pay minimum wage to workers because you can, and because that's what the "going rate" is for the type of work being performed? Or, just because you can pay the minimum wage, should you?

Not necessarily.

Consider the experience of companies like Vintage Vinyl, which built itself into the largest independent music store in the Midwest with just 23 employees. According to one of its founders, Lewis Prince, the company built its business by paying above the minimum wage. "For this small extra investment, we get long-term employees who are devoted to our company — employees whose ongoing relationships with customers have been vital to our success."[4]

Similarly, when Pi Pizzeria restaurant owner Chris Sommers raised the pay for his hourly workers to $10.10 he did it because it was good for business. Pointing out that the lower the wage, the higher the employee turnover, he explained that his company spent "more than $500 training a new line-cook. We threw away thousands of dollars in product a year due to inexperienced employees preparing it improperly. Eliminating just a portion of these expenses pays for increased minimum wages."[5]

In addition to lower turnover and lower training costs experienced as a result of paying above minimum wage, a bakery owner noted that paying above minimum wage improved the bottom line in other ways. The workers "are hardworking and efficient, and they produce a superior product with better customer service. That translates into the returning customers that drive small-business success."[6]

In 2015, large employer Aetna announced that it would move most of its workers who work in call centers to a $16.00 base hourly wage, or an average pay increase of 11%; 33% for some. At the same time, Aetna also increased its contribution and reduced some employees' contributions for health benefits. In other words, Aetna assumed more of the burden for providing health insurance for those who needed the financial help the most.

The company estimated that the cost of this increased expense would be roughly $10.5 million. However, when it calculated its total cost for turnover — from hiring and training replacements, to lost productivity and increased absenteeism — it realized it was already incurring $120 million in turnover costs per year. They reasoned a $10.5 million investment in higher wages was not a very risky investment.[7] It made sense for the business.

Finally, consider the announcement in early 2015 from the world's largest retailer, Walmart, that it would be raising its entry-level wage to $10 an hour by the following year. While Walmart has been the focus of union efforts to organize the business, the ultimate driver for an increase in the base pay wasn't union avoidance or public relations. It was driven by broader business considerations. According to Dan Bartlett, the company's executive vice president of corporate affairs, with "the changing retail landscape, with the different options that customers have, competition on prices is tougher than we've seen it in a long time, and with that comes an increased premium on experience in the store."[8] And according to the annual meeting report[9] as presented by Walmart's Chief Executive Officer, the raise in pay resulted in an increase in job applications and a reduction in turnover — both of which will help the company's bottom line.

Even if your workforce analysis tells you that you can probably find the workers you need by paying workers the minimum wage, your analysis isn't really complete. You have to fully consider and calculate what the impact would be if you paid workers more. You may very well find that the cost savings from reduced turnover and reduced training expenses, combined with the additional revenue generated by more knowledgeable and loyal workers, provides a strong business case for paying employees more.

In other words, just because you can pay minimum wage, doesn't mean you should.

TIPPED EMPLOYEES

Unless they've worked as a waiter or waitress, most people don't realize that the federal minimum wage for employees who earn tips is only $2.13 an hour. Although some states have higher minimum wage requirements, a significant number of tipped workers are subject to this $2.13 minimum.

And because federal law permits employers to pay at this rate, many do. After all, it's what the law provides, it's what competitors pay, and if the employer is able to find workers at that rate, why not do so?

But is that necessarily the most profitable approach an employer can take?

Some restaurants, though very few, have adopted another approach, whereby they have put a "no tipping" policy into effect, and pay their wait staff above the federal minimum wage. This approach, which is largely followed in Europe where tipping is not customary, is being used by Packhouse Meats, a restaurant in Kentucky.[10] The owner has "No Tipping" on the menu, "to protect the servers, and by protecting the servers, reduce turnover."[11] Sushi Yasuda, an upscale restaurant in New York City, got rid of tips for wait staff, telling diners that "following the custom in Japan, Sushi Yasuda's service staff are fully compensated by their salary."[12]

While this may increase the cost to the restauranteurs, they have determined that the added cost is offset by savings in reduced turnover of the wait staff. New staff doesn't have to be recruited or trained, and there's no loss in productivity because of someone learning on the job.

Other restaurants have opted to not only continue allowing tipping of the wait staff, but have used technology to increase the likelihood and amount of tips, thereby increasing their employees' earnings. Bills include pre-calculated amounts for various levels of tipping to make it easier for the customer to calculate a tip, or "virtual" tip jars are placed at the cash register so customers can swipe their credit cards and pay a pre-set tip amount to the servers.

These employers have recognized that *just because they have no obligation to pay tipped employees more than the amount set by law, didn't mean they shouldn't. Other options should be considered, as should the costs and benefits of alternative approaches.*

LEAVE TIME AND FLEXIBLE SCHEDULING

People are often surprised to learn that there is no federal requirement for employers to provide paid vacation leave or paid sick leave, usually because they've always worked for an employer that provides such leave benefits. According to a survey conducted by SHRM and the Families and Work Institute, almost all U.S. employers with 50 or more employees — 99% — have some form of time off with pay for their full-time employees.

Vacation time was at the top of the list, provided by 58% of organizations, followed by sick days (52%) and Paid Time Off (PTO), where employees can take time for any purpose (41%). Of those employers that do not provide PTO (59% of all employers), 87% provide both vacation and sick days.[13]

But it's difficult, even with most employers providing leave benefits, for many workers to manage their work and their personal, family obligations. Exempt workers, or those who are exempt from the employers' obligation to pay overtime for hours worked over forty in a work week, have greater flexibility in how they schedule time, because they're paid a salary, and will get paid regardless of the hours worked.

Hourly workers have an even greater challenge in managing their work life and their personal commitments; they must operate within the constraints of a 40-hour work week — where every hour worked is recorded to ensure they're properly compensated. And being properly compensated is often critical for an hourly worker's financial stability.

Many employers maintain set hours of work because of the demands of the customers, and the need to guarantee coverage of the business. Set schedules are often also adopted because that's the way it's always been done, in the belief that it provides greater ease in payroll management —

the hours are set and all employees must work within the schedule. Sometimes employers insist on all workers having the same schedules to avoid appearances of favoritism or because they worry that allowing deviation from the schedule for one employee will result in other employees seeking similar exceptions. Employers want managers spending their time on other priorities, not juggling staffing plans by constantly trying to meet individual scheduling requests.

But just because an employer is entitled to dictate the schedule for its workers, does it always make sense to do so?

Where schedules were once maintained on a black board in a break room or posted on a bulletin board, today's technology provides many more ways to build schedules, including self-scheduling, where work groups can self-manage their schedules. This can be done to ensure that the coverage an employer needs is provided while also giving workers flexibility to build a schedule that best fits their personal needs.

In hospitals, for example, it's critical that patients have nursing care 24 hours a day. For many hospitals, this means constant juggling of schedules, moving nurses between units when there is a shortage of coverage, providing incentive payments to cover extra shifts, or paying outside temporary nurses for coverage.

One Georgia hospital[14] implemented self-scheduling, putting the scheduling into the nurses' hands. The result was better coverage for the hospital's patients, while eliminating the need for outside temporary nurses and incentive payments for extra shifts. Nurses were willing to pick up extra shifts and fill staffing holes because they could control their own schedules.

And instead of having to be in the break room, or at work, to manage the schedule, cloud and web-based tools allow employees to manage their schedule from anywhere, at any time. The result is greater employee engagement, reduced turnover and absenteeism, and better coverage for the employer.

Some call centers have also had great success with allowing self-scheduling of employees. Recently Zappos, an online shoe retailer based in Las Vegas, began piloting technology that allows workers to self-schedule a portion of their work, and which would compensate employees based on a surge-pricing model.[15] Those hours that have greater call volume would be compensated at a higher rate. While still in development (employees receive points towards prizes instead of surge-pay), the goal is to provide employees greater autonomy and control over their schedules, while providing the employer with improved coverage for the call center.

Just because you can exercise total control over employees' work schedules, doesn't mean you should.

EDUCATION AND TRAINING

One of the first things to be eliminated from a budget during tough economic times are dollars that are set aside to provide employees with professional development opportunities. Businesses, faced with challenges to their very survival, will eliminate any expense that doesn't quickly provide some return on the investment in the form of increased profitability.

There are no laws that require employers to provide employees with training designed to enhance the worker's career opportunities. In fact, the only training mandated by law tends to be around ensuring worker safety or preventing workplace discrimination.

But should an employer provide professional development and training to employees anyway? Many do, because doing so benefits the business in many ways, including:

- Increasing productivity — Employees who receive training to do their job are more likely to be more efficient and better able to handle customer issues and concerns.
- Helping in recruitment efforts — Candidates are much more likely to accept a position in which they believe they can grow and develop, assisted by the employer.
- Helping with retention — Employees who receive some educational assistance benefits are much less likely to leave an employer.
- Increasing employee engagement — When employees feel well equipped and trained to do their job they are likely to be much more engaged in their work, and employee engagement can drive profitability.

Federal tax law allows employers to take a business deduction for expenses to provide tuition reimbursements to employees, up to $5,250 a year.[16] In addition, this reimbursement for tuition expenses is not considered taxable income to the employee. Many employers provide tuition reimbursement programs, but limit their commitment to the tax protected amount.

New technologies and advances in distance learning are making employers with large hourly workforces, which often don't provide college education assistance or only provide limited assistance, reconsider.

Perhaps most widely publicized is the recent announcement from Starbucks. Under what Starbucks has called the "Starbucks College Achievement Plan," all 140,000 U.S. based part- and full-time employees can have their entire tuition towards a bachelor's degree paid for when obtained through online courses offered by Arizona State University.[17] Estimated to cost the company $250 million by 2025, the effort is not simply one designed to reflect the Starbucks' brand of being a socially responsible company or because the Chief Executive Officer knows the value of education to workers. It was done knowing that this benefit will attract and retain workers in a tightening labor market, while also advancing the brand.

Similarly, Fiat Chrysler recently announced that it is launching a program to cover the cost of college degrees for those who work at Chrysler, Jeep, Dodge, Ram Truck, and Fiat dealerships. Available to 118,000 workers in the U.S., the program will offer associate, bachelor, and master degrees through Strayer University's Degrees@Work program, and do so free of charge to the employees.

According to its press release announcing the new program with Strayer, Fiat Chrysler launched the program because it felt that "offering free college degrees without the burden of debt presents a significant value that we are pleased to provide and that differentiates us from our competitors. It will certainly help us attract and retain strong talent."[18]

In 2015, McDonalds also increased its benefits (and pay) offerings to its workers, announcing that it was increasing its existing program to help McDonalds' employees gain more education by expanding its "Archways to Education" offerings to include free high school completion and college tuition assistance.[19]

All of these brand name companies have recognized that providing some level of educational assistance makes business sense by both enhancing their brand and reducing costs incurred by turnover, recruitment, and training expenses.

They've realized that just because a company doesn't have to provide any educational assistance, doesn't mean it doesn't make business sense to do so.

THE VALUE OF THE EMPLOYER/EMPLOYEE RELATIONSHIP

These examples — paying minimum wage, compensating tipped workers, providing leave time and flexible scheduling, and providing education and training — are but a few areas where employers can adopt employment practices that simply meet the minimum requirements of the law. But employers should always keep in mind the relationship they want to have with their workers, and how that relationship can affect the business' profitability.

And always remember, that just because an employer can do it — pay the minimum, do nothing to provide flexibility, or do nothing to help workers gain training and education — doesn't mean they should.

At a small holiday gathering with her co-workers, Bobbie was surprised to receive a holiday bonus approved by the district manager. The handwritten card said, "In thanks for your continuous service and the joy you deliver to our customers." That wasn't the only surprise.

Bobbie's supervisor announced that the entire staff would be receiving pay increases on January 1st, and that many full- and part-time employees would begin to "accrue" paid time off. For a full-time employee like Bobbie, that meant she could earn up to 40 hours in a year to stay home if she or one of her children became sick. The room buzzed with excitement. Bobbie smiled. Now she could get Ronnie the art set he wanted.

ENDNOTES

1 https://www.osha.gov/oas/trianglefactoryfire-account.html

2 http://www.ncsl.org/research/telecommunications-and-information-technology/employer-access-to-social-media-passwords-2013.aspx, retrieved June 7, 2015.

3 http://en.wikipedia.org/wiki/Minimum_wage_in_the_United_States, retrieved June 8, 2015.

4 http://www.usnews.com/opinion/blogs/economic-intelligence/2013/08/09/a-fair-minimum-wage-helps-workers-and-businesses

5 https://blog.dol.gov/2015/04/07/chris-sommers-boost-business-by-raising-minimum-wage/

6 http://www.businessforafairminimumwage.org/news/00772/philadelphia-inquirer-amy-edelman-minimum-wage-increase-helps-workers-employers

7 http://www.strategy-business.com/article/00324?pg=all

8 http://www.washingtonpost.com/blogs/wonkblog/wp/2015/02/27/why-wal-mart-decided-to-finally-pay-its-workers-more/

9 http://www.reuters.com/article/2015/06/05/us-wal-mart-stores-shareholders-staff-idUSKBN0OL2IL20150605

10 http://www.packhousemeats.com/wp-content/uploads/2015/01/ph_food_menu_0115.pdf

11 http://thinkprogress.org/economy/2014/06/10/3446937/packhouse-meats-tips/

12 http://thinkprogress.org/economy/2013/06/11/2134891/new-york-sushi-restaurant-eliminates-tipping-because-they-pay-waiters-a-salary-with-benefits/

13 http://familiesandwork.org/downloads/paid-leave-nse.pdf

14 http://www.healthleadersmedia.com/page-1/NRS-277930/SelfScheduling-a-Win-for-Nurses-Hospitals

15 http://fortune.com/2015/01/28/zappos-employee-pay/

16 http://www.irs.gov/publications/p970/ch11.html

17 https://news.starbucks.com/collegeplan

18 http://www.media.chrysler.com/newsrelease.do;jsessionid=5529B4C34B36A1C96424E83A4349ADDA?&id=16539&mid=

19 http://news.mcdonalds.com/press-releases/mcdonald-s-usa-announces-new-employee-benefit-package-including-wage-increase-an-nyse-mcd-1185520

Section 3

HELP YOUR PEOPLE DO THEIR BEST EVERY DAY

Bobbie has worked at a popular hotel in her city for more than 10 years. She's held a variety of roles, and is currently an assistant manager in the hotel's fine dining restaurant. Bobbie has been happy in her job until recently, when a new manager was hired from outside of the organization. "I've spent a lot of years here, and I know how to provide a great customer experience," thinks Bobbie, "so why am I training yet another new manager instead of moving into the role myself?"

CHAPTER SIX

Creating a Learning Culture

Sharlyn Lauby, SPHR, CPLP
Author and Publisher, *HR Bartender*
President, ITM Group Inc.

Organizations and employees want the same things and they need each other, although sometimes it's hard to see it that way. Employees want to work for great companies that they are proud of. And they are serious about finding them. According to research from Glassdoor.com,[1] applicants are making time to research organizations before they apply to make sure they really want to work for the company before completing an application.

Companies want engaged, productive employees. They want employees who will come to work, give their best, and contribute at a high level. However, employee engagement is at a record low according to a study from Quantum Research.[2]

The way organizations can bridge the gap is by creating a learning culture — an organizational culture that encourages employees to grow, learn, and improve themselves every day. Employees feel proud that the company is setting them up for success and investing in their future. Organizations are happy to have employees that represent their brand well and deliver excellent service.

Every organization has their own unique culture and an organization's brand is defined by customers. It can be viewed as a continuous loop:

Strong organizational cultures create positive employee engagement. Engaged employees deliver good customer service. Happy customers help create a valuable brand. Respected brands achieve results that help maintain strong culture. The first step is creating the right culture.

CREATING A LEARNING CULTURE

The concept of a learning culture was first introduced by Peter Senge, PhD, senior lecturer at the MIT Sloan School of Management and author of *The Fifth Discipline: The Art and Price of the Learning Organization*. In this book, Senge outlines five disciplines that must be mastered in order to successfully become a learning organization[3]:

1. **Systems thinking** is about understanding how individual things relate as a whole.
2. **Shared vision** allows employees to understand and buy-into the organizational vision.
3. **Mental models** permit the organization to promote open dialogue.
4. **Team learning** focuses on having a knowledge management structure.
5. **Personal mastery** emphasizes individual commitment to learning.

As employees we might not have influence in all five of the disciplines that Senge mentions, but the one we do have control over is personal mastery. Whether it's designing our own personal development plan or helping an employee with theirs, we have the ability to support learning.

Given the fast pace of today's business environment, learning has never been more important. And while we say that everyone needs to be a lifelong learner, it's time to take that comment one step further. Yes, we must be lifelong learners. But we must also be keenly aware of how we like to learn and what valuable content looks like.

ADULT LEARNING PRINCIPLES

To have some understanding of how individuals like to learn, it's necessary to understand the principles of adult learning. Here are three key principles to consider:

1. **Adult learners must be motivated.** Adults already have a lot of knowledge and expertise. So for learning to be successful, it needs to be something that the individual wants to learn. The topic must be relevant and interesting.

2. **Adult learners must be self-directed.** They need to have a say in their own learning activities. When an individual understands how they learn best, they can decide if they want to learn via a book, or a podcast, or a conference. They have control and responsibility for the information.

3. **Adult learners want problem-centered content versus subject-centered.** Learning must fix a problem or help to achieve a goal. Learning cannot take place for the sake of learning. This ties into the other two principles. Individuals must be motivated to fix the problem or achieve the goal. And they need to feel that the learning will help them control their career.

Building a learning culture gives organizations engaged employees and a competitive advantage. The good news is that learning doesn't always happen in a classroom. As Dan Schawbel pointed out in his chapter in this book, young professionals and technology are showing us new ways to learn and grow professionally.

Traditional and Modern Learning Methods

Dan Schawbel also shared with us the profile of the next generation of workers. Not only do we have to think differently and use different methods when it comes to recruitment and retention, we have to change our mindset where learning is involved.

Traditional workplace learning has been in the classroom. In the Association for Talent Development (ATD) 2014 State of the Industry Report, instructor-led classroom training continues to be the most popular method of training (at 55%). However, that's changing. Self-paced and mobile training account for 32%, which explains the new trend in training called "flipping" the classroom.

The concept of flipping the classroom means that the time actually spent together is focused on activities and discussion. Activities that can be done independently, such as reading or watching a video, are completed outside of the classroom. This aligns with giving employees control over their learning so they can achieve personal mastery.

Another method, eLearning, which saw some success in the 1990s has paved the way for "micro learning" where content is distributed in bite-size snippets of 3 – 5 minutes. This method is extremely popular because it takes into account the way we read computer screens today.[4]

Organizations are also recognizing the value of informal learning. While informal learning has always existed, businesses are making intentional decisions to create and cultivate an informal learning environment. This might take place in mentoring or buddy programs. It could also take place in collaboration software platforms.

In his book, *The New Social Learning*, ATD Chief Executive Officer Tony Bingham defines social learning as "learning with and from others." He notes that it's not a delivery system like eLearning or mobile learning. I bring this up because, in some ways, everything we learn is in some form or fashion "with and from others." Whether we learn in classrooms, using our tablets, or watching a video, we learn from other people. Regardless of the method and the delivery system, being people-centric in learning is essential.

Defining Training, Development, and Learning

Now that we've established that learning is all about the learner, it's important to understand why the learning is taking place. This might seem like semantics but training, development, and learning mean different things.

> **Training** is the action of teaching a person a skill or behavior. Typically for use in their current position. Examples include software skills training or in the case of our employee, Bobbie, we could use the components of proper wine service. Within training, there are knowledge, skills, and abilities.

> **Knowledge** is the theoretical or practical understanding of a subject. For example, Bobbie might have knowledge of the wine making process or proper steps to open a bottle of wine. This doesn't mean that she has the knowledge to be a sommelier. Frankly, it doesn't confirm that she knows how to open a bottle of wine. It means she

knows a process or the steps.

Skills are the proficiencies developed through training or experience. Using the same example, Bobbie has demonstrated skills in opening a bottle of wine through serving customers in the restaurant. Skills are usually things that have been learned. So, we can develop our skills through the transfer of knowledge.

Abilities are the qualities of being able to do something. There is a fine line between skills and abilities. Some people would say the differentiator is whether the thing in question was learned or innate. In the Bobbie example, I think we could say that describing the aroma and taste of a wine to customers is an ability that would help sell more wine in the restaurant (and yield Bobbie better tips!).

Development is the action of teaching a person a skill or behavior for use in a future position. For Bobbie, this might be a supervisory skill such as interviewing. Like training, development has knowledge, skills and abilities.

Learning is the acquisition of knowledge or skills through experience, study, or training. A common example of learning is via internship programs.[5] Internship programs serve a purpose for both the organization and the individual. For companies, it gives them an opportunity to work with young professionals and gain insight about what's being taught in today's colleges and universities. It allows companies to work with someone who they might want to hire someday. And it gives an organization the opportunity to help students start their professional careers with relevant work experience (a.k.a. learning).

So training and development are learning. But learning doesn't always happen via training and development. Learning can take place in hallways, break rooms, and parking lots. That's why we need to know when training is the right solution.

Knowing When Training is the Answer

Training is not the answer to every problem. It might sound odd hearing that from a training professional and it sounds odd saying it. But when training is applied at the wrong time, it gets a bad reputation.

Here's an example. Let's say the vice president of operations runs into your office. She complains that managers can't seem to get work done on time. She tells you that she wants time management training. Can you put together a time management training program? Of course. Do we know that the reason managers aren't getting stuff done is poor time management? Not really.

Some people will conduct training just because senior management asked for it. And maybe it's rare that senior management is asking for training. But what if the training doesn't fix the problem? Six months later, during a meeting, someone says the word "training" and that same vice president says, "I don't think training brings value. I asked for training to help me with an issue and it didn't fix the problem."

What people hear: "Training doesn't fix problems." And companies become reluctant to devote time and resources toward something that doesn't appear to fix problems.

As tempting as it may be when we get the call asking for training… if it's not a problem that can be fixed with training, the answer should be "no." So, how do you figure out if training is the right solution for a problem? Ask these three questions: 1.) Does the employee have the skills to do the job; 2.) Does the employee have the desire to do the job; and, 3.) Is the employee being allowed to do the job. Here's how to interpret the results:

- If the answer to all three questions is "yes," then training is NOT the answer. It could be an equipment problem.
- If the answer to question #1 is "no," training may/may not be the answer. The solution could also be performance coaching.
- A "no" for question #2 could mean you may have an employee motivation or engagement challenge.
- And a "no" for question #3 might be the result of a policy or procedural issue.

These three questions will tell you if the issue can be properly addressed using training. Then, if training is really the answer, the company can start working on an assessment to figure out where employees currently are and where they need to be. The key is figuring out if the company should even be doing a training assessment in the first place.

It's Cheaper to Train than Recruit

Sometimes, we can apply the principles of business marketing to the concepts of recruiting and retention. For instance, I learned a long time ago that it's cheaper to keep the customers you have than to continuously attract new ones. That's not to say companies shouldn't always try to get new customers. But there needs to be a focus on retaining the customers you have for two reasons: 1.) The company has already spent the cost to acquire them; and, 2.) The company has invested the time and other resources to create brand loyalty.

Businesses stay focused on keeping customers by knowing the cost of acquiring a customer and the customer's satisfaction with their product and/or service. In addition, they know the cost of losing a customer.

Occasionally, customers leave for all the *right* reasons. For example, when they outgrow the needs of a product or service. In those cases, they often remain raving fans of the company — because that company helped them grow and succeed.

The same philosophy applies to employees. When a company hires an employee, they invest a lot of time, energy, and resources in sourcing, advertising, interviews, offers, etc. Then the new hire goes through orientation and onboarding. They might participate in other kinds of company training, like compliance training or customer service training. Their supervisor spends time talking with the employee about performance expectations, departmental policies, and more.

My guess is the company has thousands of dollars invested in this new employee. In fact, recent research from Bersin by Deloitte indicates the average time to hire an employee is 52 days at an average cost of $4,000.[6]

So when that employee makes a mistake, instead of immediately thinking warnings, discipline, and possibly termination, maybe we should consider coaching, mentoring, or additional training. After all, the company already has a lot of money invested in this employee.

Like customers, sometimes allowing an employee to leave the company (whether that's voluntarily or involuntarily) is exactly the right thing to do. Maybe the company can't give them what they need. Letting an employee pursue their professional goals, even if it means having them leave the company, could turn them into a raving fan for your business.

Managers might say it's frustrating and time consuming to fix employee situations and customer complaints. On the surface, it might appear easier to find another customer or hire another employee. But if the organization has already made the investment, isn't it worth taking a moment to look for alternatives to abandoning the relationship?

How to Calculate Your Company's Cost Per Hire

In 2012, the Society for Human Resource Management (SHRM) in partnership with the American National Standards Institute (ANSI) developed a universally accepted calculation for cost per hire (CPH):

$$CPH = (EC + IC) / THP$$

CPH = cost per hire

EC = external costs for all outside sources of spending including third-party agencies, advertising, job fairs, travel, drug testing, background checks, signing bonuses, etc.

IC = internal costs such as recruiting staff salary and benefits, time cost for hiring manager, infrastructure fixed cost, government compliance, referral bonuses, etc.

THP = total number of hires for the time period being evaluated

The Connection between Training and Recruiting

Being able to attract and retain the best talent is a top issue for organizations and the C-suite. The business world is competitive and a company's talent can be a key strategic advantage. This applies not only to acquiring the best talent but also to ensuring that talent remains the best through learning opportunities.

As the recruiting market becomes more challenging, a company has to decide the best way to find talent. There's a terrific book called *Build, Borrow or Buy: Solving the Growth Dilemma* by Laurence Capron and Will Mitchell.[7] While the book focuses on acquiring talent during organizational growth, the same principles apply when an organization is just trying to find the best talent — period.

Companies have three options to choose from: buy, build, or borrow. They can "buy" talent — meaning hire someone as an employee. They can "build" talent — which involves training employees to assume those responsibilities. Or they can "borrow" talent — suggesting that they would find a freelancer or consultant to do the work.[8] There are advantages and disadvantages to each.

Option	Advantage	Disadvantage
BUY the talent necessary to be successful (i.e. hire an employee)	A new employee brings fresh eyes, skills (ideally), and ideas to the organization.	Depending upon the position, it can be expensive not only to find the candidates but also in terms of salary, relocation, perks, and bonuses.
BUILD the talent within the organization (i.e. train employees to do the work)	Investing in current employees can have a positive impact on corporate culture.	Training takes time. This has to be considered.
BORROW the talent when needed (i.e. find a consultant or contractor)	This is a great option for specialty or niche work and can be very cost-effective.	It's important to keep even "on-call" talent engaged. Otherwise they won't be there for you when you need them.

Ultimately, the decision to build, borrow or buy comes down to two factors: time and resources. Organizations with limited time might not be in a position to build talent. Companies with limited budgets might not be able to buy the talent they need.

Since companies want to have options when it comes to talent, they need to start thinking about training and recruiting together rather than as two separate functions. The current and future skills of their employees are at stake. Planning is key. If an organization wants to build their own talent pipelines then they have to start planning for how they are going to actually do that. It might involve replacement planning, succession planning, talent pools, training resources, dedicated training staff, etc. You get the point.

The companies that will win the talent wars are the ones that will have the most options. They will build, borrow, and buy talent to their strategic advantage. They won't let time or resources dictate the outcome because they're planning for it right now.

> KEY TAKEAWAY #1:
> It costs a tremendous amount of time, money, and other resources to bring employees into the organization. Creating a work environment that allows employees to learn and grow professionally is a smart investment. Use training and development opportunities to keep employee skills relevant and create a strategic advantage for the organization.

Designing Effective Training

So far, we've talked about what training is and when it should be used. Let's say, after those steps, we absolutely know we need to conduct training. Now what happens? Well, as Mark Wales pointed out in Chapter One, we need to create training objectives that align with operational goals.

There's an easy and effective way to develop a training objective. It's called the A-B-C-D method, where A = Audience, B = Behavior, C = Condition, and D = Degree. As an example, Bobbie is going to attend a supervisory skills training program to learn how to conduct interviews. The training objective for the program could be:

> *Participants will learn how to conduct a fully-compliant behavioral interview based upon the book,* 96 Great Interview Questions to Ask Before You Hire *by Paul Falcone.*[9]

Using the A-B-C-D method, the audience is Bobbie and the other participants. The behavior is conducting a behavioral interview. The condition is based upon the book *96 Great Interview Questions* and the degree is fully compliant. The objective is specific and clear. Participants know what to expect. Bobbie's supervisor knows what to expect when Bobbie returns from training.

Once the objective is created, then the program can be designed. Don't let training design scare you! Here are five steps to designing a training program that works for any size group.

1. **Welcome the participants and establish the WIIFM (What's in it for me?).** The goal is to make participants feel comfortable and safe. Tell them why this training is important and how they will be able to use it — a key principle of adult learning.

2. **Share knowledge and expectations.** This is a good time to understand how much participants already know about the topic as well as
   what they want to come away with as a result of attending. As a
   trainer, you want to relate to the audience. Understanding their level
   of knowledge and their expectations is essential.

3. **Discussion and/or demonstration**. In the case of Bobbie attending
   behavioral interviewing training, this is the portion of the program
   that will focus on telling participants how to construct behavioral
   interviewing questions, interviewing dos and don'ts, etc. The
   training might also include a video demonstration of the proper way
   to conduct an interview.

4. **Testing and practice.** Participants get the opportunity to practice in
   a safe environment. They can ask questions, conduct role play, and
   become comfortable with the content.

5. **Feedback and debrief.** To wrap up, the group can have a discussion
   about the things that went well and the things they might do
   differently in the future. This gives them the ability to learn from
   each other and to confirm understanding of the information.

Now honestly, there's a bit more (actually, quite a bit more) to designing
training than that. But this basic outline is great for conveying a piece of
information and making sure people understand it. The outline works especially well in a one-on-one setting. Have a conversation with the employee,
let them try the skill, then meet with them to debrief. It also works in
department meetings. Using our initial scenario, Bobbie's supervisor could
show everyone how to decant a bottle of wine at a shift briefing.

The reason I like this five-step approach to training is because it removes
barriers. Training can easily happen with few resources. In today's business
world, we keep hearing about the importance of being a lifelong learner.
Well, if we make training difficult to do and expensive to produce, we limit
learning opportunities for employees, and we prevent the company from
having a learning culture.

In addition, employees must do more than be lifelong learners to remain
relevant. They must have a clear understanding of how they like to learn
and what good content looks like. For instance, is the best way for Bobbie
to learn how to conduct a behavioral interview by listening to a podcast on

interviewing techniques? Or is it reading a book on the best interview questions to ask? Or is it co-interviewing candidates with someone in human
resources? Or maybe yet… it's a combination of all three.

Development Opportunities

Pew Research reports that every day 10,000 Baby Boomers will turn retirement age (65 years old).[10] And in 2015, the Millennial generation surpassed
Boomers as the largest living generation.[11] What this means for organizations is that their older workers will be looking to scale back and eventually
phase out of the workforce. Organizations need to be prepared for this
transition in terms of developing younger workers and planning for the
transfer of historical knowledge.

Earlier in this chapter, we defined development as learning for future
opportunities. There's never been a more critical time to think about the
future workforce. As Boomers plan their exit strategies, organizations need
to have employees ready to assume those responsibilities.

> **Replacement planning** is a short-term focused activity to identify
> individuals (usually internal) that would assume roles should an
> opening occur. For instance, if the accounting manager announced
> their resignation tomorrow, who would take over their responsibili-
> ties? In the case of Bobbie, if a lead server or restaurant manager left
> tomorrow, would Bobbie be ready to take on that role?
>
> **Succession planning** is a long-term view to identify individuals
> (internal or external) for future openings. Remember the build,
> borrow, or buy strategy we discussed earlier in this chapter? It's a
> similar concept. Companies have to decide if they will hire or
> develop future talent. Should the company develop Bobbie so she
> can become the next restaurant manager?

One of the biggest challenges with replacement and succession planning
— besides actually doing the exercise — is making decisions about how
much to share with employees. Do you tell an employee they are part of the
succession plan? I tend to lean toward the yes camp, telling employees they
are part of a succession plan can be a retention tool. Employees know that
they are valued and the company wants to make an investment in their

future. If an employee's performance starts to suffer, then hold the employee accountable.

However, I do see the view of the other side. Some say no, because it might give an employee a sense of entitlement which could make things difficult if an employee's performance goes below the company standard. One way companies can have the best of both is by creating talent pools.

A talent pool is a means to identify future candidates and give them the development they need without identifying a specific future opportunity. So an organization can create talent pools to give employees management and leadership development and let the employees know they are important to the future of the company, without being specific about the job/position/title.

Coaching and Mentoring

Another method for developing talent that also allows for the passing of knowledge is through face-to-face interactions. Coaching and mentoring are two common ways of doing this. While sometimes the terms are used interchangeably, the activities are very different.

> **Coaching** is focused on listening, questioning, and process. A coach's methods are directed toward action plans, goals, and accountability. Their aim is to help someone achieve a goal that's been set.

> **Mentoring** is typically done between two individuals, where one person is considered a subject matter expert in the topic they are mentoring. This method involves teaching and development. The mentor is passing along their knowledge and skills.

One method is not superior to another. Both coaching and mentoring have their unique advantages. Organizations are able to provide employees with coaching and mentoring based upon their needs. For example, if Bobbie has a skill or knowledge gap, providing coaching could be an effective way to help her develop an action plan to address the situation. On the other hand, if Bobbie knows she wants to work in the restaurant industry, but is struggling with moving up to the front of the house versus the back of the house, a mentor might be able to provide direction.

> KEY TAKEAWAY #2:
>
> Training and development makes employees effective in the jobs they do today and the ones they will do in the future. Organizations have the opportunity to show employees their value and how they impact the bottom-line, which is a key driver of employee engagement and retention.

The Role of Technology in Learning

Technology plays an important role in our lives. Learning is no exception. In Chapter 2, Bob Clements reminded us that using technology effectively can increase the time we spend on higher value tasks and rewarding work. One way we're seeing this is in the form of just-in-time learning.

Here's the premise: let's say we're Bobbie and, 99% of the time, restaurant guests order cocktails or moderately priced bottles of wine with their meal. On rare occasions, a table will order an expensive bottle of wine, which requires decanting.[12] Instead of focusing our energy on remembering the details of decanting, we focus on delivering excellent service to the 99% and when someone orders a wine that needs decanting, we're able to watch a two-minute video in the kitchen that explains how to properly decant a bottle of wine.

Take this one step further. We're a sales person who spends the majority of our time in the field. A customer asks about a very specific feature on a product. The sales person can use their smartphone or tablet to retrieve the answer. Whether it's on a PC in the kitchen or on our mobile device in a customer meeting, we get the information we need, just in time.

Technology also brings tremendous freedom to the learning environment. In today's highly competitive business world, it's a challenge to schedule employees for full-days of training. Not only is it a challenge to the operation, but it can be a challenge for the employee — especially if they work remotely. Just-in-time and mobile learning allow employees the freedom to learn within their existing schedule.

Gamification

Another way that technology is shaking up the learning environment is with gamification. It's defined as using game thinking and mechanics in a non-game context. The advantage to gamification is the fun factor that game elements bring to the learning experience. The challenge is making sure that the game achieves its goal or business result.

In the book *For the Win: How Game Thinking Can Revolutionize Your Business,* Kevin Werbach and Dan Hunter share several examples of organizations that created leaderboards, badges, and points systems (common game elements) but weren't able to create sustainable behavioral change because ultimately, the "game design" was flawed. The leaderboards, badges, and points attracted attention initially; but, because the goal wasn't defined, users quickly lost interest.

So creating games in the context of learning is wonderful, if it is done properly and with a goal in mind. A good example that keeps with our Bobbie case study is My Marriott Hotel.[13] The goal of this game is to provide a virtual environment that simulates the real work atmosphere. It gives users insight into what it takes to run a hotel.

In an article for Mashable, I had the chance to ask a Marriott executive how the game works. First, players manage a 'virtual' hotel restaurant kitchen. They buy equipment and ingredients on a budget, hire, and train employees, and serve guests. Points are earned for happy customers, lost for poor service and ultimately, players are rewarded when their operation turns a profit. Then they are able to move on to other areas of hotel operations. Not only is the simulation fun, but it serves a purpose. It gives outsiders a glimpse of the complex operations that take place inside a hotel. With this perspective, users are able to decide if working in the industry is right for them.

Measuring Training Effectiveness
Giving participants the ability to offer feedback is one way of measuring training effectiveness. In the example of My Marriott Hotel, Marriott says that at any given time, people from more than 120 different countries are playing the game, which is pretty incredible, since Marriott doesn't operate in 120 countries.

A more formal method of training evaluation was developed by Donald Kirkpatrick in 1954. In the model which bears his name, the four-levels of training course evaluation are:

1. **Reaction:** This refers to what participants thought of the training. A common example is the evaluation form provided at the end of training sessions.

2. **Learning:** This evaluation represents the increase in knowledge as a result of training. An example would be if the trainer gave participants a test to see their level of knowledge at the beginning of class then again at the end of class.

3. **Behavior:** This measures the transfer of knowledge to the job. The trainer might observe participants at their work location to see if they are using the information from the training.

4. **Results:** These are the final results that occurred as a result of the training. It might be increased sales, decreased defects, etc.

Finally, the last way to measure the effectiveness of training is to weigh the costs of the program to its benefits. According to SHRM, the formula for measuring return on investment (ROI)[14] is:

ROI = Program Benefits / Program Costs

If the ROI is greater than 1, then the benefits outweigh the costs and the program is considered effective. If the ROI is less than 1, then the costs of the program exceed the benefits.

If the goals and objectives of training are clearly connected to business goals, then typically the ROI is achievable. It might take some tweaking to the program costs, but it is attainable. And the good news is that today's learning environment provides plenty of options to help organizations meet their training goals.

Organizations that embrace learning create cultures that encourage employees to improve their skills and develop themselves for future

---

KEY TAKEAWAY #3:

Effective training and development opportunities provide employees with the skills they need to be successful. When training and development is offered using methods that employees find interesting and engaging, the return on investment is realized both in terms of program delivery and organizational results.

---

opportunities. A learning culture provides effective training that employees want to attend. It offers development programs that give employees a sense of belonging so they will stay, ensuring the company's pipeline of talent is filled with qualified individuals. And, creating a learning culture helps an organization maintain its competitive advantage in this fast-paced business economy.

Bobbie's new manager has settled into his job and is spending a lot of time talking to the staff about how they can make the restaurant even better. He is impressed with Bobbie's knowledge and ideas, and has begun implementing some of them. Even better, he's talking to her about specific steps she can take to position herself for a manager role. Between his coaching, and the training plan they've developed, Bobbie believes that her goal of becoming the manager some day is achievable. When a rival restaurant across town calls her about an assistant manager position, she decides to stay put.

ENDNOTES

1 http://www.hrbartender.com/2013/recruiting/job-seekers-research-companies-
   before-applying-friday-distraction/

2 http://www.quantumworkplace.com/infographic-employee-engagement-trends-
   nation-hits-8-year-low/

3 http://www.hrbartender.com/2014/training/interview-peter-senge-education-
   systems-thinking-careers/

4 http://www.parentcenterhub.org/repository/web-reading/

5 http://www.hrbartender.com/2013/recruiting/10-must-haves-for-a-successful-
   company-intern-program/

6 http://employers.glassdoor.com/blog/why-are-companies-taking-longer-to-fill-
   positions/

7 http://www.amazon.com/Build-Borrow-Buy-Solving-Dilemma/
   dp/1422143716/ref=sr_1_1?s=books&ie=UTF8&qid=1432775187&sr=1-1&key
   words=build+borrow+or+buy+solving+the+growth+dilemma

8 http://www.workforceinstitute.org/category/recruiting/

9 http://store.shrm.org/96-great-interview-questions-2nd-edition.html

10 http://www.pewresearch.org/daily-number/baby-boomers-retire/

11 http://www.pewresearch.org/fact-tank/2015/01/16/this-year-millennials-will-
   overtake-baby-boomers/

12 http://www.winespectator.com/webfeature/show/id/45882

13 http://mashable.com/2012/07/27/business-games/

14 http://www.shrm.org/education/hreducation/documents/09-0168%20
    kaminski%20roi%20tnd%20im_final.pdf

"Sorry for the blast." Bob hated to start an email like that, but it had become customary whenever someone sent an "all company" request for information. As a technical sales lead in a professional services business providing payroll and tax filing services, Bob relied on his peers for answers when he received inquiries on integrating with niche systems or on how to configure the occasional outlier legislative rule. Some recent turnover had thinned the ranks of Bob's usual go-to resources, and he was responding to a big RFP. He recalled Bill from services addressing the specific integration question "Exodrome" asked, but Bill was gone and Bob couldn't find the email. Bob stared at his inbox. The RFP was due tomorrow.

CHAPTER SEVEN

Collaboration Creates Value: Social Technology in the Workplace

Jeanne Meister
Partner, Future Workplace, LLC
Kevin Mulcahy, MBA
Partner, Future Workplace, LLC

INTRODUCTION

"In the long history of humankind (and animal kind, too) those who learned to collaborate and improvise most effectively have prevailed."

— Charles Darwin

The Current State

Employees across all generations believe working for a company that makes collaboration a priority is becoming an important criteria for finding an employer. According to a 2014 MIT Sloan Management Review Study entitled *Moving Beyond Marketing: Generating Social Business Value Across the Enterprise*, roughly 57% of survey respondents say that social business sophistication is important in their choice of employer. That attitude is consistent among respondents aged 22 to 52.[1] Thus, across a range of ages, there are more similarities than differences in what people want in the workplace and in their careers, and one of them is the ability to work when and where they need.

Some companies are even making progress on this! According to a 2014 Randstad survey on business collaboration, 61% of employees now spend more time collaborating with colleagues than they did five years ago, and 74% stated that their employer should spend more time on promoting collaboration.[2]

The Opportunity to Drive Greater Collaboration

A major transformation is underway in how employees are choosing to get their work done. Workplace expectations have evolved to the point that employees are no longer likely to move any project forward without getting the input of others. Interacting, sharing, and collaborating at work are increasingly being enabled with social functionality through the use of new tools ("technological shifts"), design of space ("physical shifts"), and shifting attitudes and behaviors ("psychological shifts"). Taken together, these shifts increase organizations' incentives to build more open, socially collaborative cultures that drive organizations towards increasingly group-centric, and decreasingly individual-centric, working cultures.

Collaboration is fundamentally about how employees engage on what they need to get done, with whom, where, and how those interactions are enabled. Being an effective social collaborator is becoming a recognized new skill necessary to becoming a high-impact contributor in the workplace. Effective social collaborators build trust through authentic and personal relationships enabled by mobile- and cloud-enabled devices anyplace, anytime, from multiple platform choices. Done well, social collaboration enables a highly engaging and productive social business and work experience.

Collaboration at scale and speed is a new skill for many in the workforce. Future Workplace has researched this topic and found a number of common themes regarding the perceived benefits and barriers, as well as the business implications for building a collaborative culture. The goal is to create effective social collaboration, which can democratize ideas and opinions, and push traditional hierarchies to robust knowledge sharing.

The Benefits of Leveraging Social Collaboration in Organizations

Many employees still see room for improvement in how collaboration happens in the workplace with two in five employees claiming that there is still not enough collaboration in their workspace according to a Randstad survey.[3] In fact, 60% of respondents reported performing better in a team than when they work individually, 66% said that people are innately collaborative, and 89% agreed that working in teams requires specific social skills.[4] The benefits of leveraging social collaboration in organizations include:

Improved Knowledge Sharing to Increase Employee Engagement

- Real-time and crowd-sourced feedback facilitates productivity and reduces the risk of poor decisions and wasted time in tracking down the right resources. It also allows experts to solicit trustworthy intelligence to help them make business decisions.
- Social collaboration tools enable employees to engage internal subject matter experts and tap into the collective knowledge of the company.
- Collaborating stimulates companies to become better learning organizations, helping employees to grow individually and as teams within the company.

Improved Speed of Innovation

- Social collaboration engages employees to rapidly distribute information, generate ideas, and invent new solutions and approaches. It challenges organizations to inventory their human capital differently and introduces a mechanism to highlight individual competencies so others can understand why people would engage or find the people that they want to engage with, based on objective recognition of individual expertise by the organization.

- The tools are forcing organizations to explicitly address the questions of "How do we enable employees to identify what they know? Who they know? What are they best at? What they are known to be best at?"

Improved Engagement from Structured Collaboration

- Social collaboration tools engage employees to contribute to their corporate community.
- Research studies from Gensler to Steljes to Cornerstone OnDemand cite the benefits of working in a collaborative fashion.

A 2014 workplace survey cited by Gensler, an American design and architecture firm headquartered in San Francisco, found that employees "often combine or toggle between focused and collaborative modes throughout the course of a typical workday," and 41% spend their time collaborating, either spontaneously or in formal meetings.[5] This is reinforced by Steljes research which finds businesses with effective collaboration practices are 5.3 times more likely to reduce risk in decision making, 3.1 times more likely to speed innovation, and 2.3 times more likely to make quicker and more informed decisions.[6]

CASE STUDY EXAMPLE: How Unisys Increases Productivity through Social Collaboration

A growing number of companies talk about the benefits of collaboration, but the list of companies actually adopting collaborative workplace practices for increased business results is far shorter. Unisys, a global information technology company with more than 20,000 employees, has quickly made collaboration part of its culture in an attempt to become more agile, share knowledge, and increase the speed of innovation.

One of the biggest barriers to collaboration is a disconnect between the aspiration to become collaborative, and the reality of being a closed organization. Former Unisys Chief Executive Officer Ed Coleman addressed this through leading by example. He became an early adopter of collaborative tools to communicate with employees, and in the process, he became a role model for adoption among both his senior executive team and the larger employee population.

Gloria Burke, Director of Knowledge Strategy & Governance at Unisys, along with co-directors John Knab and Rajiv Prasad, launched "Inside Unisys," a knowledge-sharing and social network internal to the firm. Coleman began blogging and soon his senior executives encouraged their teams to do so as well. Employees are automatically alerted to blog and microblog postings on the newsfeeds on Inside Unisys. Over time, Unisys salespeople began using Inside Unisys to share information about recent wins as well as share lessons in losses.

Creating a collaborative knowledge-sharing environment is not the responsibility of one department. "People support what they help to build," says Burke. "And, once it is built, they have a stake in its success." She set up an advisory council with senior leaders from across the company — business units, HR, IT, Legal, Finance, Marketing, and more — to create a shared vision on how "going social" would improve employee and organizational productivity.

To be really useful, social collaboration has to improve the daily work of employees. Knowledge workers can spend a significant amount of time seeking to obtain the information they need. So when Unisys launched "My Site" to allow employees to build their personal credentials and network of colleagues, they built a feature called, "Ask Me About," which allows Unisys employees to locate experts across the organization by creating hashtags for their skills and key topics so all employees and their skill sets became "searchable," making collaboration easy and accessible. In the first 18 months after the launch of Unisys My Site and the searchable feature, 15,000 Unisys employees worldwide (out of 20,000) built profiles and created hashtags describing their expertise.

Senior executives studied the early adopters and tracked adoption rates in monthly meetings. These rates were then compared against the well-known Rogers Adoption Curve of Innovation classifying adopters of innovations into five categories based upon their willingness to try new ideas. The key lesson: if a company wants to build a more collaborative culture, start with innovators and early adopters and others will follow as they see the benefits of using social media in their work.

Collaborating Virtually and Physically

Distributed work teams mean that people who really enjoy their jobs are able to do them anywhere in the world. Forward looking companies are building new physical and digital spaces to create environments where people can come and collaborate and share ideas. These spaces are enabled by a range of tools needed to support alternative workplace choices.

What we see with Future Workplace clients is the increasing ability for companies to build choice and flexibility into where and how employees work. In fact, work no longer needs to occur in a fixed place and time, and is instead more of a mindset focused on getting a job done. As connected and collaborative technologies become more readily available, employees have the option to work anywhere and any place they can be productive.

But there is a skill associated with how to work collaboratively. Online chats need to be "tagged" to virtual projects. And for certain workflows, moving communication onto an online collaboration platform can allow for a more integrated approach to team communication and more efficient task management within distributed teams.

Collaboration Styles Can Differ by Culture, Role, and Generation

There appear to be differences emerging in the communication modes preferred by different generational cohorts. For example, Boomers and older Generation X working adults continue to prefer using phone and email for direct conversations, while Millennials are more comfortable with the instant communications of text messaging, group online chats, or multiple forms of visual and collaborative media. Many members of Generation Z, our youngest generational cohort, will have grown up with the daily interactions of social networking, video-based communication, instant messaging, and real-time presence. Several will have been educated in classrooms using interactive whiteboards, as well as using tablet-based learning resources to access homework portals where they downloaded homework instructions and uploaded completed homework products. They will bring to the workplace a natural temperament for collaboration and will expect their employer to provide the latest tools to co-create and participate in design thinking projects as part of their workflow.

But the challenge for companies is not to organize employees into generational cohorts and expect a certain type of work behavior. Instead, companies need to move beyond one-size collaboration stereotypes and think about building collaboration profiles based upon an employee's role and function within the company. One example of this is provided by Cisco, where the company has proactively developed Employee Personas and started to segment employees based upon their collaboration work styles, such as:

- *Workstation Anchored:* Desk-bound, non-mobile employee who performs highly focused individual work; some team interaction
- *Remote Collaborator:* Non-mobile employee who works frequently with remote colleagues, and frequently works from home
- *Campus Mobile:* Internally mobile; interacts cross-functionally in face-to-face scheduled meetings; often in leadership roles
- *Neighborhood Collaborator:* Neighborhood-based employee who is

mobile within the group area; interacts with, coordinates, and manages teams

- *Highly mobile:* Travels extensively to customer and partner locations; frequently interacts with customers

Our advice to companies is to think beyond age cohorts, develop an understanding of how work gets done, and use this knowledge to create a collaboration workflow for various job roles.

Company Collaboration Technologies Are Only as Good as the Culture They Enable

Social collaboration technologies are fundamentally transforming the way people work together, learn, and communicate in the workplace, but these new platforms are only as good as the culture of collaboration they enable. Tools are not the generators of collaboration. The collaborative drive needs to arise before the technologies are put into place and then employees will need to be properly trained on the mix of collaborative technologies. Case in point:

LEADING COLLABORATION TOOLS BEING USED IN THE MARKETPLACE INCLUDE

- Cisco Spark: Allows team members to create rooms with group messaging, content sharing, video calling, and desktop sharing.
- Yammer: Microsoft's private social network for employee collaboration within enterprises.
- Lync: Microsoft's instant messaging and audio conferencing software designed to integrate with the company's Office 365 products.
- Chatter: Salesforce's social collaboration and file-sharing service.
- Jive: An out-of-the-box collaboration tool with a user friendly interface.
- IBM Connections Suite: Suite that provides IBM social software, real-time social communications and content management capabilities in a single offering
- Slack: Offers real-time messaging, archiving, and search for users to streamline communications and share documents.
- Flowdock: A group chat service for teams that integrates with popular social media and productivity tools.
- VMWare Socialcast: A mobile collaboration platform, with social networking, video distribution and management, and content management.

the Randstad Survey on Collaboration found that, while 87% of respondents believe collaboration is increasingly important with the advancement of technology, only 60% indicated their employer provides tools and training to facilitate working in virtual teams.[7] This disconnect between investing in collaboration tools and providing employees with the training needed on how to use these tools in the workplace will make the difference between the winners and losers in the race to embed collaboration in the workplace.

Moving the Social Collaboration Agenda Forward

Implementing social collaboration for business results is just like any other new initiative — it starts with the development of a business plan, an analysis of strengths, weaknesses, opportunities, and threats, and a plan of action to identify early use cases where leveraging social collaboration will result in delivering business impact to the organization. In consulting with many organizations on their social collaboration strategy, we have found five ways to move the social collaboration agenda forward:

Identify the business problem to be solved and the key executives who will embed social and collaborative ways of working into the workflow of their teams. In the case of Unisys, their Chief Executive Officer and senior leadership team were the first to become active in *Inside Unisys,* their corporate intranet. They saw the business benefits for the entire organization, as well as an opportunity to increase the productivity of a particular group — the sales team.

Communicate the hard business benefits of bringing social networks into the enterprise — not just the soft ones of increasing knowledge sharing. No one will be moved to better understand social collaboration if you simply tout the knowledge sharing benefits. Instead, focus on explaining the hard business benefits, including the potential for increases in employee productivity, enhancements in finding information to solve a business issue, and improvements in time-to-market for a new product or service. Focus on sharing performance results of the impact of social business in the workplace. For example, *The Social Economy Report* authored by McKinsey

Global Institute found that knowledge workers spend 37% of their work week reading and answering email while looking for answers to business needs.[8] This totals 650 hours a year. Most importantly according to McKinsey research, social technologies, when used within and across enterprises, have the potential to raise the productivity of knowledge workers by 20 to 25%.[9] So, far from being a distraction, using social tools in the workplace can be a boon to productivity.

Create social collaboration literacy training programs so everyone understands how to share knowledge in a safe and respectful manner. If you closely examine the list of commonly mentioned barriers to social collaboration, confusion over what it means to be social will be at the top. One of the ways a growing number of organizations are addressing this is by developing social collaboration literacy programs. This is already happening in a broad range of companies and industries.

Recognize the diverse collaboration needs of different employee personas for both onsite and online collaboration. For example, as part of its *BlueWork Program*, American Express conducts an employee survey, which helps assign employees to one of four categories: Hub, Club, Roam, and Home. "Hub" employees' work requires a fixed desk, and their presence in the office every day. "Club" employees have flexible roles that involve in-person and virtual meetings; they have the opportunity to share time between the office and other locations. Those in the "Home" category are based from home offices — set up with assistance from the company — on three or more days per week. "Roam" employees are almost always on the road or at customer sites, and seldom work from an American Express office. "The ability to work in a flexible work-space is based on the role you have, not personal preference," said Jose Morabito, a Vice President of Finance and member of the "Club" group at American Express. It's significant that American Express designates employees' work categories based on careful consideration of each role and employee persona. This careful study of each role and how work gets done enables collaboration to be seamlessly woven into the workplace.

Define new roles inside the Human Resources function starting with identifying and training online Community Managers who will manage the online communities that will be created as a result of adopting social business. The Community Manager must be a savvy power user of new collaboration technologies with strong editorial and online moderation skills, and a passion for community engagement.

The expectation is that employees will increasingly expect to bring their digital lives to the workplace and to use their employer's internal social networks for working, learning, and communicating. Social collaboration tools now appear to fully meet that requirement. In the future, the ability to manage communities may become a core leadership attribute for leading collaborative enterprises of the future.

Six months after his company lost the Exodrome deal, Bob received another RFP with the same unique integration requirement. Fortunately, six months prior, after his old colleague Bill had returned from his vacation safari, he returned Bob's call and walked him through the solution. Bill

also told Bob about the collaboration software they used at his new company. The Exodrome loss helped Bob convince his management to invest in the collaboration software, so now a simple search turned up the answer that Bill had provided and that Bob had entered into the knowledgebase. The company was growing and the collaboration tool not only helped employees find and catalog answers, but it helped the many remote employees get to know each other a little better. And "sorry for the blast" became a thing of the past.

ENDNOTES

1 Gerald Kane, Doug Palmer, Anh Nguyen Phillips, David Kiron, Natasha Buckley.
   "Moving Beyond Marketing: Generating Social Business Value Across the
   Enterprise." July 14, 2014. Accessed at: http://sloanreview.mit.edu/projects/
   moving-beyond-marketing/ (June, 24, 2015).

2 Judith Franssen. "Randstad Workmonitor Wave 3." September 2014. Accessed at:
   http://www.randstad.com/press/research-reports/randstad-workmonitor/
   randstad-workmonitor-collaboration-at-work-sept-2014.pdf (June 24, 2015).

3 Judith Franssen. "Randstad Workmonitor Wave 3." September 2014. Accessed at:
   http://www.randstad.com/press/research-reports/randstad-workmonitor/
   randstad-workmonitor-collaboration-at-work-sept-2014.pdf (June 24, 2015).

4 Judith Franssen. "Randstad Workmonitor Wave 3." September 2014. Accessed at:
   http://www.randstad.com/press/research-reports/randstad-workmonitor/
   randstad-workmonitor-collaboration-at-work-sept-2014.pdf (June 24, 2015).

5 Metropolis Editors. "Everything about the Way We Work is Changing. Here's
   How." June, 2015. Accessed at: http://www.metropolismag.com/
   June-2015/A-to-Z-Everything-about-the-Way-We-Work-is-Changing-Heres-How/
   (June 24, 2015).

6 Speech given by Tim Price_Walker, Steljes at Worktech™ 14, London, November
   2014.

7 Judith Franssen. "Randstad Workmonitor Wave 3." September 2014. Accessed at:
   http://www.randstad.com/press/research-reports/randstad-workmonitor/
   randstad-workmonitor-collaboration-at-work-sept-2014.pdf (June 24, 2015).

8 Michael Chui, James Manyika, Jacques Bughin, Richard Dobbs, Charles Rox-
   burgh, Hugo Sarrazin, Geoffrey Sands and Magdalena Westergren. "The Social
   Economy: Unlocking Value and Productivity through Social Technologies." July,
   2012. Accessed at: http://www.mckinsey.com/insights/high_tech_telecoms_in-
   ternet/the_social_economy (June 24, 2015).

9 Michael Chui, James Manyika, Jacques Bughin, Richard Dobbs, Charles Rox-
   burgh, Hugo Sarrazin, Geoffrey Sands and Magdalena Westergren. "The Social
   Economy: Unlocking Value and Productivity through Social Technologies." July,
   2012. Accessed at: http://www.mckinsey.com/insights/high_tech_telecoms_in-
   ternet/the_social_economy (June 24, 2015).

Section 4

CONTINUOUS IMPROVEMENT
AND INNOVATION

Bob, a young foreman in a specialty metal fabricating plant, shows us why analytics are both interesting and practical, and perhaps most importantly, why they are better at helping us articulate and solve problems than the "gut instincts" or "hunches" we often rely on. The stories in this chapter illustrate analytics and evidence-based decision making from the viewpoint of a young foreman.

CHAPTER EIGHT

Tales of Everyday HR Analytics

David Creelman
Chief Executive Officer, Creelman Research

INTRODUCTION

When we hear the phrase "HR analytics" it sounds very... well, very uninteresting. You may also think it's a technical subject, suitable only for people who find statistics fun. However, analytics starts with the simple willingness to say "I don't know. Let's find out." You don't need to be an analytics expert to have that mindset.

Carnegie Mellon's Denise Rousseau likes to say: "Make decisions based on the best available evidence." This sounds so reasonable that you wonder why professors would bother writing books about it; but data shows that even in medicine, doctors often base decisions on their personal opinions, not the best available evidence.

The Telltale Donut Bags

Bob was no Sherlock Holmes, but his curiosity was piqued by the piles of donut bags in the trash at the far end of the plant. The nearest donut shop was a 15-minute drive away. A round trip would surely take 45 minutes end-to-end. How did anyone have time to get donuts?

Time was a big deal for him. The team he was directly responsible for was sweating buckets to keep up with the production schedule. They cut and polished parts and they were always rushed at the end of any big job, especially if there was re-work. Bob had hinted to the factory manager that he needed more staff on this line, but the glare she had given him was enough to send him scurrying back to check on the delivery of some new equipment. There, near the shipping dock, one of the old hands waved him a welcome. "Hey new guy, want to go on a donut run?"

Bob answered, "Thanks, but my team is running behind. How is it that you guys have time to go for donuts?"

"The enamel's cooking. We gotta wait until that's done, no point sitting around staring at the oven."

Bob saw that there were indeed several workers sitting around; something that never happened in his unit... well, except on the days when they realigned the machines or were between big orders.

Bob couldn't go for donuts, but he could ask why it was that in some parts of the plant there was excess labor while in other parts there was too little. When he got back to his end of the plant, he demonstrated a key trait of the analytical manager: curiosity.

He asked one of the other foremen, "Tony, why the heck are there a bunch of guys sitting around at the other end of the plant while we're running ragged here?"

Tony explained that scheduling workers across the plant was a complicated issue; especially since workloads were volatile and not everyone could work in every area.

Tony looked up towards the office perched overlooking the plant "Man, I remember when I started, the scheduling guy had all these piles of papers and he managed to get it all figured out in one day. He was a bloody genius."

"Don't we have computers for scheduling now?" asked Bob.

"Yeah, maybe, sure, actually I know we do... heard about it."

Now it was Bob's opportunity to go back to the factory manager, "I think I know how we can speed up production."

Bob was no analytics expert, but he knew that the factory was, as a matter of course, collecting a ton of data in their time and attendance and scheduling system. Surely, given what modern software can do, it should be possible to optimize the shifts so that when some units were overstaffed labor could be shifted to units needing extra hands. The scheduling software would need access to the data on who had the skills and certifications to work in different units, but all that was available.

The factory manager, who clearly remembered the guy who could do scheduling with nothing more than a pile of papers, wasn't sure of the capabilities of their new scheduling software, but a call to the vendor suggested it wouldn't be hard. In fact, the vendor said it would probably be a simple problem compared to the scheduling they did in hospitals with 24-hour shifts and a wide range of technical specialties.

It turns out the vendor was right. The scheduling system was not being used to anywhere near its full capabilities. It took some work, but it proved possible to significantly increase throughput by optimizing the scheduling. Add in some cross-training and the scheduling software was able to easily match talent to need, shift by shift. The only problem was in the donut shop, where the staff found themselves standing around wondering why their customers weren't coming as often.

What's the lesson here? Sometimes what matters is just an awareness of what analytics can do. Bob never touched the scheduling software, but it was apparent to him that there were underutilized resources, and lots of data about who was working on what for how long. He saw the opportunity for optimization, and made the effort to ask how analytics could help the factory. Just as the capabilities of phones have increased immeasurably, so too the ability to gather and analyze workforce data has sped ahead of our understanding of what is possible.

The University of Dilbert

Bob was in big trouble. There was a new manager in the regional office and one of the first reports he had looked at was absenteeism. The absenteeism numbers in Bob's unit this quarter were bad, in fact the worst in the region. The new manager thought it would be a good signal to the other foremen to give Bob the boot.

Analytics, which had helped raise Bob's reputation by optimizing labor usage, were coming back to bite him. Was he really the worst manager in the region? His "gut" told him no, but of course, part of the point of analytics is to replace gut feel with data. Luckily for Bob, an evidence-based approach is a little more subtle than just ignoring gut feel. If we ask the question this way, "Bob, as someone close to the absentee issue in your department, do you, in your expert opinion, think there is a serious problem or not?" he would have said that yes there has been absenteeism, but it was for good, if odd, reasons, like the carpenter who had pulled a muscle from sneezing too hard; it wasn't due to Bob's bad management.

Bob had not studied statistics but he did remember a Dilbert comic where the boss was complaining that 40% of absences occurred on Mondays and Fridays — implying people were taking days off to enjoy a long weekend. It took him a moment, but he realized the joke in the comic strip, there are only 5 days in a work week so naturally you would expect 40% of the absences to occur on any two of them.

The University of Dilbert led him to formulate the question this way: "Is it reasonable to assume the high absenteeism is just the statistical variation, in essence a string of bad luck, rather than being caused by lousy management?" Here Bob had stumbled on one of the most important concepts in analytics: pose an answerable question.

He wasn't sure that a Dilbert comic was a sufficient source of evidence for that "answerable question," so he contacted his personal adviser and explained his logic.

"My gut says it's not my fault... and then there's this Dilbert cartoon."

She replied, "That's your argument??"

"I'm still fine tuning it, that's why I'm talking to you."

"Well, what is it that leads your gut to think it's not your fault? What have you observed?"

"My team is happy. You can tell when people are fed up and are getting payback by taking extra time off. I don't see that in my team."

"So your model is that low engagement is a causal factor in inappropriate absenteeism and your observations show engagement is high, leading you to doubt bad management is causing the absences."

"Yeah, that's it."

"What else?"

"Well, I know my people have been away a lot but there are good reasons. I mean three of the team had their homes flooded when the river backed up; that accounts for a bunch of absences. I know a lame half-baked excuse when I hear one; these excuses are legit."

"So your model is that inappropriate absenteeism, which can be a result of bad management, is accompanied by a poor quality of excuse, but we are not seeing that indicator — your observation is that excuse quality is high."

"Yeah, like I said."

That was enough, Bob had his model and the next day at work rushed to explain it to his boss. At first his boss just looked at him, then he spoke up. "That stuff about models, causal factors and indicators, it's not you talking. It's Janet, right?"

"Janet?"

"Janet, your wife, the actuary, the one with bad taste in men."

"Yeah, maybe a bit, it was a collaboration."

"Never mind, this hypothesis that it might be a normal fluctuation makes some sense. You should get Janet to run the numbers," he joked.

Once Bob had framed the question this way he still had a big problem. If he did the analysis showing the absenteeism was just a statistical variation then he'd prove he was right and the new regional boss was wrong. Given the realities of organizational life, this would probably be a worse outcome than being seen as a lousy foreman who can't control absences.

This was a couple of pay grades above Bob so he had to be strategic. One day, Bob said to one of the engineers "Hey, want to go for a donut run?"

Arriving at the strangely quiet donut shop, Bob explained his theory, that if you looked at the probability of the string of absences it would not be unexpected, and things would regress to the mean in time, and there'd be no need to fire Bob. The engineer understood immediately; and shortly after found the opportunity to drop some hints to the new regional manager. The regional manager then thought up the idea of doing a deeper analysis, and thanks to this diligence found that Bob's bad numbers this quarter were probably just a fluke. Bob kept his job, and the regional manager was lauded for his sophisticated analysis of data.

As Bob discovered, one of the downsides of HR analytics is that people may take a shallow look at the data and think it proves the case definitively. Data can mislead. One of the principles of evidence-based management is that data doesn't give you the answers, it just informs judgement. Furthermore organizational data is just one source of evidence, others include academic studies, expert opinion, and stakeholder views (see sidebar for an explanation of the latter). Bob's gut feel was, in a way, expert opinion, although it had to be unpacked with some careful questioning to make it credible.

How do you balance organizational data against other sources of evidence such as expert opinion? One of the explicit steps in evidence-based practice is appraising the weightiness of each piece of evidence. In cases where the data is poor and the expert has a deep understanding, then expert opinion probably gets more weight. For example, if you are judging where to locate a

> ## STAKEHOLDER VIEWS AS EVIDENCE
> One of the seemingly odd things in evidence-based management is the idea that stakeholder views count as a form of evidence. It doesn't mean that if the speedometer says 50 and the stakeholder says, "We're only going 30," that the stakeholder is right. However, stakeholder views are relevant if the question is not, "What speed are we going?" but, "What speed is safe?" One risk of analytics is that we dive in and get the answer to the wrong question. We always face the risk that our own views are too narrow. By explicitly including stakeholder views as one of the forms of evidence, we reduce the risk of overeager numbers-junkies who don't have adequate understanding of the organizational context leading us astray.

new retail outlet based on foot traffic as the sole data point, versus an expert's opinion that the location won't be viable, then it might be prudent to give the expert's opinion more weight. On the other hand, if carefully collected data shows that placing a product on the right side of the store leads to higher sales than on the left, then the data is probably weighted higher than the store manager's opinion. The takeaway is that analytics bring better insights to the table so that we can make better decisions, but they are not meant to blindly replace informed human judgement with equations.

The Case of the Crummy Cutting Tools
Our last vignette takes place on a Friday when Bob walked by two of employees "discussing" different means of improving throughput.

"This cutting tool is garbage, at my last company we used the Japanese ones," said one worker.

Her colleague didn't buy it. "You just don't know how to use the tools, we've always used this brand."

"You're out of date, sometimes you have to spend money to make money. We'd save on the re-work."

"It wouldn't make a difference, I've been in this business 20 years, you don't know...."

Bob intervened, "I see you are discussing a hypothesis about cutting tools, what does the data show?"

The workers reacted to the words "hypothesis" and "data" as if Bob was speaking Greek and Latin; but after Bob explained what he meant, it quickly became clear that there was no data to be found.

That phrase "What does the data show?" is one of most beautiful ones in evidence-based management. It is topped only by the Bob's next phrase, "Let's find out."

Bob's idea was to rent the more expensive tools for a month on one line, and keep the usual tools on the other line. They were already tracking throughput and re-work so it would be an easy matter (for one of the engineers) to do the math on whether the more expensive tools were paying off.

It wouldn't be a perfect experiment that proved beyond a shadow of a doubt which choice was better; but it would provide reasonably good evidence that would let them make an informed decision. Certainly it was better than arguing. The other smart thing Bob did was set this up as a proper experiment by looking at throughput before and after the test runs and by having the control group using the old tools. He might have just said, "Let's try the new tools and see how it goes," but that wouldn't have produced good data the way a well-thought-out experiment would.

Bob figured that the higher quality tools would pay off, but the data showed the old guy was right: the cheaper tools were almost as good and the numbers didn't justify switching. The result surprised Bob, but the bigger surprise was how his team reacted. They were really excited about how a worker suggestion for improving productivity had been taken seriously and how the "Let's-find-out-mindset" helped everyone get past their own personal opinions. In the year ahead the team had lots of ideas about little things they could do to improve productivity, they'd back up their suggestions with evidence, and all those little things added up to big gains in throughput.

Lessons Learned

The essence of HR analytics and evidence-based practice is moving away from opinion and argument to simple questions like, "What does the data show?" or, "What is your hypothesis?" or, "What question are we trying to answer?" or, the ever useful, "Let's find out!"

You don't need to have a degree in statistics to be an evidence-based manager (or foreman), you just need a scientific mindset. You often do need access to people with deeper analytical skills and analytical tools (like the tools embedded in the advanced scheduling software that Bob used to balance workload), but those skills and tools are readily available, probably within your own company.

There is something of a myth that analytics will give you the right answer, just like you got the right answer in a grade 10 math test. In business, it's not like that. We often can't get solid proof either way, but we still need to make a decision, so we make it on the balance of the available evidence. If it looks like one cutting tool will be better than another based on a careful consideration of the available evidence, then that's the one to buy. That's a far better way to make a decision than making the choice based on a strong but data-free opinion.

Evidence-based management doesn't exclude expert opinion as a valuable input, but expert opinion is most convincing if you can tease out the hidden reasons that lead the expert to their conclusion. Bob actually had some pretty sound reasons behind his expert opinion that the high absenteeism was just a statistical aberration; however until those reasons were unearthed it sounded like he was just looking for an excuse.

Experiments are a key part of evidence-based management and we don't do them enough. The word "experiment" may sound formal, but it really just means testing something out and learning if it works. However, if you do "try it out" in too casual a way, then the evidence you gather won't be convincing. In the case of the cutting tools, Bob ran one line with the old tools and one with the new tools so they could make an accurate comparison. If an experiment is particularly important then it would make sense for a guy like Bob to find someone in the company, or maybe a university professor, who has enough of a scientific background to design a reasonably rigorous experiment.

Perhaps another myth that is held by people trained in analytics is that all they need to do is gather and weigh the available evidence and management will happily accept their conclusion. This might work on the planet Vulcan, but it doesn't happen that way on Earth. Organizations on this planet are full of humans, and humans don't react to evidence the way Spock would. They don't like surprises, they don't like to be shown to be wrong, and they don't like decisions to be made without their involvement. Bob's colleague in engineering showed sensitivity to organizational reality in how he gently got the new regional manager to see if the absenteeism problem was just a statistical aberration

One of the most impressive things about Bob's organization is hidden from view. This organization had a culture that created the conditions where analytical thinking could flourish. Employees were engaged and wanted to see improvements. The management was open to listening to employees and changing things. There was enough slack in the system that there was time to do some thinking and some experiments. Contrast this to companies where employee initiative is not encouraged or where everyone is so insanely busy that they never have time to reflect or learn or improve. The science of analytics rests on a base of culture, and you need both for an organization to benefit from the power of evidence-based practice.

Bob is pleased with the wins he has had lately at work as a result of taking a data-driven approach to pushing for changes. The leaders at Bob's organization are likewise pleased with Bob. Their commitment to creating a learning organization, listening to new ideas, and providing their  employees with the opportunity to innovate is paying dividends for everybody. Bob has decided that he'll take an online course in LEAN principles and maybe even go for his Six Sigma Black Belt. Maybe he could even be plant manager someday if he keeps asking the right questions.

Bobbie has a director level position at a respected high-tech firm. She's well compensated and her benefits are competitive. She also absolutely hates going to work every day. There's a big gap between her organization's values as stated in the ubiquitous posters on the walls of the company headquarters and the behaviors that her senior leaders exhibit. That gap leads to divisive behaviors throughout the company that benefit neither employees nor customers.

"I've got to find another job," thinks Bobbie, "one where I can really make a difference."

CHAPTER NINE

Engaging Leadership in Setting the Winning Game Plan
China Gorman
Consultant, Speaker, and Author
Former Chief Executive Officer, Great Place to Work® Institute

A Chief Executive Officer ahead of his time, Jack Welch believed that the team with the best players wins. More and more Chief Executive Officers understand this to be true today and are shifting their thinking, focus, and behavior to lead in ways that reflect this belief. But what is the role of the C-suite in creating this winning environment? What can and should leadership do to support the shifting of intention to a more people-focused culture that, as Jack Welch modeled, will not only win in your competitive business landscape but will also win on the ultra-competitive talent landscape of today and tomorrow?

These aren't idle questions. On June 4, 2015 *Fortune* posted the results of the 2015 *Fortune 500 Chief Executive Officer Survey*. The top five business challenges cited by these Chief Executive Officers might surprise you:

1. The rapid pace of technological innovation
2. Cyber security
3. Increased regulation
4. Shortage of skilled labor
5. Management diversity

Two of the top five challenges identified by the Chief Executive Officers of the Fortune 500 are talent-related. The systemic challenges of attracting, hiring, developing, retaining, and deploying talent are becoming top of mind for Chief Executive Officers and their C-suites all over the world and in companies of all sizes. And so, Chief Executive Officers and

Chief Human Resource Officers (CHROs) are working more closely together than ever before.

The strategies introduced in this book lay out evidence-based, successful approaches that will empower employees to deliver winning performance for your customers, your business, and their own lives. In the main, these are proven, on-the-ground practices where the rubber meets the road — organizational systems and solutions that enable great engagement by, and productivity from, employees. But let's take a look at the C-suite's role in leading the creation of a highly-engaged, winning culture.

ESTABLISH A VISION FOR THE FUTURE
Trustworthy Leadership
Leadership's role in creating a vision for employees is a critical responsibility. We all know this. But being a credible and trustworthy leader is the first step in everything a leader does. When employees don't trust their leaders to be fair, competent, respectful, and appreciative, everything is more difficult and results are hard won. Trustworthy leaders are approachable, they communicate honestly, and they express appreciation for the efforts of their employees.

It is quite remarkable how "thank you" can begin to build that trustworthy foundation. One newly appointed Chief Executive Officer I know had two very visible behaviors that set her apart from her predecessors: she learned the names of all the employees at the corporate headquarters and made it a point to address them by name in the elevator, in the parking garage, just walking down the hall. Additionally, as she traveled the globe, she had prep materials that introduced the employees at each location: names, titles, pictures, reporting relationships — so she could address those employees by name as well. Taking the time to do this showed great respect and appreciation for her colleagues.

She also sent handwritten notes of appreciation to employees who reached performance milestones, who had service anniversary dates, and who participated in task force or committee work. She sent those thank you notes to the employees' home addresses so family members would see how appreciated those employees were.

Two small gestures with enormous personal and cultural impact resulting in creating a strong, trusting bond between leader and employees.

Values and Leadership Behavior

Employees look to their leaders to model the stated values of the organization. If leaders are held to a different — lesser — set of norms, employees quickly see through the façade. If integrity is a core value and leaders shade their expenses; if diversity and inclusion are core values and the leadership all looks the same; if innovation is required and failure is punished; if fairness is a foundation and promotions are handed out based on favoritism; if one gender is paid more than the other for the same work — all of these communicate what the organization's values really are. If the leaders don't walk the talk, employees easily become cynical, less engaged, the quality of their work diminishes, and they may soon be gone.

Jon Persson, Chief Executive Officer of Cygni, a Swedish IT firm and a Great Place to Work® in Sweden and Europe, has said, "Nobody wants to be just a number in a budget or a spreadsheet. Everybody wants to be seen and be appreciated."[1] The belief of this Chief Executive Officer has created a culture of trust and mutual appreciation that has established a highly engaged workforce that gives its all every day. Little wonder the company's growth has been rapid.

Evidence-based Decision Making

As David Creelman pointed out in his entertaining chapter on analytics, the ability to use data-derived business intelligence for workforce planning, talent acquisition and management, and other people-related decisions will be more and more critical for organizations in the coming months and years. Chief Executive Officers require business intelligence as a foundation for strategic decision making across the board — it's just new as it relates to talent. And just as organizations have the ability to drive actionable intelligence from data, employees have more and more crowd-sourced and publicly available employer-related data to contemplate as they make choices about where and whether to engage full-time or part-time through the established corporate economy — or to be an independent contingent worker accessing assignments through the "gig economy." The proliferation of sites like Glassdoor and Great Rated! will continue to put actionable data within ready reach of workers. Chief Executive Officers want even more from their side of the equation.

Whether you're analyzing payroll data, time and attendance data, turnover data, performance management data, recognition data — or a host of other people-related data — HR must continue to look for evidence to support its recommendations to the C-suite. No more a "gut" or "soft" function, HR's impact on whether or not strategic plans get executed is front-and-center in most organizations now because of the magnitude of difficulty in attracting, hiring, developing, and deploying talent today — the talent required to execute strategy. And it's only going to get more difficult as the global workforce demographics begin to shift more rapidly in the next 10 years.

Some analysts report that a typical HR department in an organization with 5,000 or more employees has, on average, more than 18 different HR systems deployed. Typically, these systems don't talk to each other and most aren't integrated into the Enterprise Resource Planning (ERP) software. This makes collecting and analyzing people-related data difficult, but not impossible. One of the great developments of today's workforce compared to the early 2000s will be the growing ability to aggregate data from many information collection sources. Making sense of these data will enable significant insight to develop new, more effective strategies to ensure an organization has the right skills when and where they need them. This is HR's true strategic organizational value today and in the future.

Patty McCord, a former Chief Talent Officer at Netflix, relayed the following to author Christine Bader in a May 2015 article in *The Atlantic*: "You wouldn't think of going to another country or doing a new initiative or changing the direction of the company without having a Chief Financial Officer in the room to be able to model what it is going to cost. You also should not be able to think about any of those things without having the person in the room that says 'Do we have the right people to pull that off?'"[2] Having the data readily at hand to model those answers is what Chief Executive Officers need, and are beginning to require.

Reaching for the Stars or Striving for Operational Excellence: What's the Difference?

This question is reminiscent of Peter Drucker's supposed observation that "culture eats strategy for breakfast." The difference between reaching for the stars and operational excellence in most organizations is irrelevant, because senior leaders give it little thought, no action is taken, and no one is held accountable. In these organizations, operational acceptability is the norm, with excellence — when it appears — being unsustainable due to high turnover, lack of collaboration and innovation, and average performance. Organizations where a solid mission, vision, and values are the bedrock of the culture, and where leaders are open, accountable, and approachable, are better able to galvanize employees around the achievement of sustained operational excellence.

There are case studies galore from the likes of Stanford, Wharton, Harvard, MicKinsey, Great Place to Work®, and WorldBlu™ that demonstrate the business and financial value of creating a workplace culture that allows all stakeholders to reach for the stars and set new standards of operational excellence. WorldBlu™ recently published some analysis (http://www.worldblu.com/research.php) showing that freedom-centered organizations saw an average cumulative revenue growth rate coming out of the Great Recession 6.7 times greater than the S&P average during the same three-year period. In the same vein, Great Place to Work® and Russell Investment Group analyzed the cumulative stock market returns of the publicly held 100 Best Companies to Work for in America compared to the Russell 3000 and the S&P 500. Year in and year out, the 100 Best Companies provide nearly three times the return of the comparative indices. The data are solid. Operational excellence is enabled, is supercharged, by culture. It more than eats strategy for breakfast. It eats it for breakfast, lunch, and dinner — if the Chief Executive Officer and his or her C-suite are all-in on the values-based focus on culture.

Garry Ridge, Chief Executive Officer of WD-40 Company, a WorldBlu™ Freedom-Centered company, said, "Third party research has shown that companies with strong cultures and higher engagement levels enjoy better returns and stronger growth. As a publicly traded company, strong returns help ensure that we can maintain our strategic course and strength of culture, while fulfilling our responsibilities to shareholders."[3]

STANDARDIZE, STREAMLINE, AND SIMPLIFY

Efficiency and Productivity Build Individual and Organizational Confidence

While talent issues are foremost in the minds of C-suite members all over the world, so too are the usual suspects of lowering costs, raising quality, and becoming more competitive. The connections between talent issues and competitive issues are clear and becoming clearer every day. This creates great focus from leaders on selecting technology solutions that are easy to adopt and have quick payback horizons. When new solutions are quickly adopted, gains in efficiency are frequently achieved. Seems obvious, right? But leaders frequently lose sight of the efficiency/productivity motive when evaluating complex system solutions. It all comes down to the ability of users to understand, adopt, and change behavior systemically.

The ability of users to quickly move from unconscious incompetence (I don't know what I don't know), through conscious incompetence (here's exactly what I don't know), to conscious competence (I know how this works), onward to unconscious competence (I know this so well I don't have think about it) increases a new system's ability to improve efficiency/productivity. And this is where it frequently falls apart. A focus on communication, training, and coaching — no matter how far off the budget the project wanders — makes or breaks the ability to achieve efficiency/productivity gains, and certainly ensures the achievement of the original ROI goals.

Simple is Always Better than Complex

Organizations in all industries are working to utilize technology to simplify processes while increasing quality outcomes and decreasing errors. Many solutions' selection processes begin with a fundamental question: Are we making the process more or less simple and efficient? The desired outcome, of course, is less complexity and more efficiency. Otherwise, what's the point?

Smart Technology Solutions Allow More Time for Innovation and Collaboration

A recent IBM study of 1,700 Chief Executive Officers found that "Outperformers are embracing new models of working that tap into the collective intelligence of an organization and its networks to devise new ideas and solutions for increased profitability and growth." As so eloquently stated in Jeanne Meister and Kevin Mulcahy's chapter on social collaboration, harnessing the collective intelligence of an organization with clean, usable, and engaging systems can build efficiencies and productivity in every industry and in companies of all sizes.

PUT THE BEST TEAM ON THE FIELD

Talent is the Key to Everything

Without talent, a business ceases to exist. And leading the creation of a culture that is irresistible to the right people is every Chief Executive Officer's job. It's every leader's job. Being approachable and promoting open communication; being transparent, communicating a clear vision, and sharing information; demonstrating competency by ensuring language and leadership behavior match — all of these are key to creating the kind of culture that will have your employees raving on Glassdoor. These are the leadership behaviors that are talent magnets.

Walter Robb, Co-Chief Executive Officer of Whole Foods Market, which has been on the Fortune 100 Best Companies List every year since 1988, said, "Companies have to continue to invest in their culture, just like they would invest in any asset."[4]

What the Generations Have in Common

Much is being made of generational differences in the workplace today, as laid out in Dan Schawbel's earlier chapter in this book. And it's true that different generations were socialized differently. Baby Boomer leaders learned how to lead in a more hierarchical organizational context: "We operate on a need-to-know-basis around here and I'll tell you what you need to know." Generation Xers were socialized in a much more diverse and socially aware context: "Corporate social responsibility and a focus on doing well by doing good" became a strong and motivating dynamic. And Millennials were socialized through the first waves of social transparency in the workplace enabled by social media and mobile devices: "Working anywhere, anytime rather than everywhere all the time" has changed the fundamental employer-employee relationship.

These socialization differences notwithstanding, everyone — regardless of age — wants to work for leaders they trust, leaders they respect, and leaders who appreciate them and are fair. Everyone — regardless of age — wants to be proud of their work and proud of the brand they work for. And everyone wants to enjoy the people with whom they work. Researchers all over the world validate these findings. And so, while socialization patterns may be different by age demographic, the deepest motivations of all are remarkably similar. The takeaway for leaders? You can never say thank you enough. You must provide work experiences that matter and give meaning to employees' lives. And creating a talent acquisition and management function that attracts people who fit the intentional culture and organization values — with no compromises — must be a key priority.

The Best Talent Flocks to the Best Leaders

It's true: The best talent wants to work for the best leaders and with the best colleagues. Great Place to Work® recently published a report detailing what differentiates the companies on the 2015 *Fortune Best Companies to Work For List*. A Twitter employee was quoted as saying, "They hire the brightest and the best here and it's enjoyable to come to work every day and surround [my]self with and learn from these people. In terms of adding value to my career, Twitter is bar none the best organization that has done so." In that same report, an employee of Edward Jones said, "I'm convinced that we continually strive both individually and as a firm to put our clients first. I've never done anything like this before, and I don't intend to go anywhere."[5]

Both of these employees are describing their own personal experience as employees in great workplace cultures. But both employees acknowledge the role of leadership in creating their inspiring employee experiences. This is the critical takeaway for leaders: Employees want to do their best work every day but rely on their leaders to create a solid and unshakable values-based culture in which both they and their company can thrive.

HELP YOUR PEOPLE DO THEIR BEST EVERY DAY

Development is an Investment, Not a Cost

In 2014, the companies on the Fortune 100 Best Companies list made the following investments in employee development:

- Average annual training and development for salaried employees: 73 hours
- Average annual training and development for hourly employees: 58 hours
- Number of 100 Best Companies that offer tuition reimbursement to employees: 88
- Average tuition reimbursement available to each employee each year: $7,375[6]

These kinds of investments clearly pay off for Best Companies through reduced turnover — with as much as 65% less turnover than industry competitors, significantly higher candidate application rates, and higher stock market returns. Today, when identifying, acquiring, developing, and deploying the right talent is top of mind for the C-suite, the business case for employee development is pretty easy to make. Just ask Howard Schultz, Chairman and Chief Executive Officer of Starbucks, who announced in early 2015 that Starbucks will provide 100% college tuition coverage for all part- and full-time employees.

Leadership Development is a Sustainability Strategy

As senior leaders grapple with the impact of the imminent loss of their Baby Boomer management teams, most organizations are focusing on upskilling the next level of leaders in their organizations. In some industries fully 45% of all employees and 80% of all management-level employees are within eight years of retirement. What if they all left on the same day? Those organizations would be out of business! Thinking of talent growth and replenishment as a business sustainability strategy makes sense in an ecosystem that looks less robust today than in times past.

Ensuring the viability of the leadership of an organization certainly is a responsibility of HR leaders. But all C-suite members have a vested interest in ensuring that the show will go on without them. Developing a leadership bench, contributing to succession plans, and connecting development goals to company business strategies are the responsibilities of all leaders — not just the CHRO.

Flexibility Means Business

With more and more focus on the business benefits of ensuring employment opportunity for all, becoming as flexible as possible helps smart organizations recruit more diverse employees. While it's true that not every job lends itself to telecommuting, and many service jobs require employees to be on the job in person, nearly every position can benefit from some type of flexibility — whether it's the use of mobile applications to punch in and out of work, the ability to work from home occasionally or every day, flexibility around returning to work after the arrival of a child or recuperating from illness, opting for compressed workweeks, offering sabbaticals or unlimited vacation or sick time — employers who are competing hard for talent are finding that offering more flexible work arrangements brings in more applicants.

And flexibility isn't just about the acquisition of new talent, it's also about the development and retention of existing talent. So organizations like Starbucks, WD-40, Ernst & Young, Accenture, Whole Foods Markets, and Cisco are innovating new ways to engage and retain their existing employees. Leaders and organizations that understand that the adoption of flexible work arrangements has a positive impact on employee satisfaction, and thereby a positive impact on customer satisfaction, are ahead of this critical curve.

Employees who Feel Successful Personally and Professionally Will Make Your Business Successful

Richard Sheridan, Chief Executive Officer of Menlo Innovations (a perennial WorldBlu™ Freedom-Centered company), was recently quoted as saying, "Employees tell us they love their jobs. The community tells us what a great impact we're having. Clients appreciate our responsive approach. When you have that many people pulling for you, great things happen."

John Chambers, longtime Chairman and Chief Executive Officer of Cisco, has said, "Our employees want to work with amazing colleagues, take pride in what they do, and expect Cisco's leaders to empower, lead, and engage with them. To do this effectively, we strive to create a workplace that not only focuses on how our employees work, but on how they live, play, and learn."[7]

The role of the C-suite in modeling organizational values, being approachable and transparent, and recognizing that their people are the key to their success has never been more important. Talent shortages, increased competition from both innovative disruptors and global powerhouses, technological advances, and demographic shifts all mean that leadership from the top has to be hyper-focused on the acquisition, development, engagement, and retention of talent. If it's true that the team with the best players wins, then these strategies will ensure that your team has not only the best talent, but the best game plan, the best coaches, and the best game-day technology. This is the winning formula Chief Executive Officers are looking for.

Bobbie loves her new job. The company is successful, due in no small part to the coherence between the members of the leadership team and their demonstrated commitment to their employees. Employees' insights are actively solicited and there are lots of opportunities to

contribute to the business. The Chief Executive Officer even sent Bobbie a hand-written thank you note the other day after a customer sang her praises in a meeting he'd attended. As she heads to her car after a long day she thinks to herself, "You can't really appreciate the value of a great culture until you've worked somewhere where it's toxic." Bobbie is committed to staying with her new company for a long time to come.

ENDNOTES

1. Great Place to Work® Institute, 2014, "Good News about Great Workplaces in Europe".

2. Christine Bader, "To Do Good in the World, Get a Better HR Department," *The Atlantic* (May 13, 2015).

3. WorldBlu, 2015, "Freedom At Work™: Growth & Resilience".

4. Great Place to Work® Institute, 2014, "Great Place to Work® Guide to Greatness".

5. Great Place to Work® Institute, 2015, "Industry Specific Strategies of Winning Companies".

6. Great Place to Work® Institute, 2014, "Great Place to Work® Guide to Greatness".

7. Great Place to Work® Institute, 2014, "The Dawn of the Great Workplace Era" webcast (http://www.greatplacetowork.com/best-companies/worlds-best-multi-nationals/watch-the-webcast).

Acknowledgements

I have a lot of people to thank for this third book in our Workforce Institute series. First, I thank my husband, Dennis, for encouraging me to take on this project, which grew out of our conversations about the relationship between employee engagement and customer service. Our authors, all members of the Workforce Institute Board of Advisors, were generous with their time and talents and created great content based on their various areas of expertise. You can find their biographies at the end of this book.

My Kronos co-workers, Domenic Locapo, Jenna Slattery, and Leo Daley all contributed their time and talents to shaping the final product. Our collaborator Tom Fishburne provided the illuminating cartoons featured throughout the book. Laura Shea Souza did a great job editing and Mady Gorrell did her usual patient job of taking our manuscript and turning it into a book that we can be proud of.

Lastly, I thank my employer, Kronos Incorporated, for providing me with the inspiration and opportunity to create the Workforce Institute and these books. When I started the Workforce Institute at Kronos in 2007, it began as a social media experiment. Since then, we've established a great network of thought leaders who have contributed hundreds of blog posts and podcasts to the cause of improving the workplace for workers, their management, and their customers. We've also created a voice in the market for Kronos that addresses the people side of workforce management.

There is a reason that Kronos wins a lot of awards for being a great place to work. I hope everybody reading this book can find a place to be similarly inspired.

About the Contributing Authors to this Book

CHAPTER ONE
MARK WALES, MBA
Vice President, Global Workforce Management

Mark Wales, Vice President, Global Workforce Management, has over 30 years of retail experience in the U.S., Europe, and Asia with leading retailers, including Ralph Lauren, Williams-Sonoma, Selfridges, and Tesco. In addition, he has provided retail consultancy with IBM and Price Waterhouse Coopers. His expertise includes implementing and driving benefit from initiatives including ERP, eCommerce, and Workforce Management. Mr. Wale's most recent focus is on developing a next generation workforce management model that drives company performance through impact to the customer experience and investment in the employee. A member of many industry advisory boards including the Workforce Institute at Kronos, Mr. Wales is also a noted industry speaker, author, blogger, and web podcaster. He holds an MBA in Retail & Wholesaling from the University of Stirling; and a BA in Social Administration from the University of Nottingham.

CHAPTER TWO
BOB CLEMENTS
Senior Vice President, Strategy, Axsium Group

Bob Clements is Senior Vice President, Strategy at Axsium Group, where he heads up this leading workforce management consulting firm's global retail practice as well as its marketing, service strategy, and other growth initiatives. Prior to joining Axsium, Mr. Clements directed product strategy for Infor Global Solutions, Workbrain, 360Commerce, and Simplified Workforce Solutions. He also held senior management positions at Orbit Commerce, Platinum Technology, and Browning & Clements. Mr. Clements is considered one of workforce management's most influential thought leaders. He led the National Retail Foundation's (NRF) Association for Retail Technology Standard (ARTS) committee to establish standards for workforce management integration. He also helped develop ARTS' Standard Request for Proposal for WFM which is widely used by retailers. Often interviewed by the press to comment on industry trends, Mr. Clements regularly speaks at industry events. He holds a BA degree in Journalism from Colorado State University in Fort Collins, Colorado.

CHAPTER THREE
DAVID ALMEDA
Chief People Officer, Kronos Incorporated

As Chief People Officer at Kronos Incorporated, David Almeda is responsible for overseeing the global human resources function at Kronos. He drives the company's human capital management strategy — including talent acquisition and development, compensation and benefits, and employee engagement programs — to support the company's continued growth, innovation, and profitability. A firm believer that innovative ideas come from Kronites who work in every corner of the globe and that a talented workforce is the cornerstone of Kronos being successful, Mr. Almeda is passionate about employee development. An active advocate for Kronites to view Kronos as a great place to work and a company committed to health and wellness, Mr. Almeda is credited with bringing the "WorkInspired" employment brand to life at Kronos. He brings a wealth of human resources management expertise to Kronos, after having spent 16 years in various human resources functions at Staples, a $25 billion retailer with more than 90,000 employees worldwide. No stranger to managing functions across vast geographic regions, Mr. Almeda's most recent position with Staples was Vice President of Global Human Resources. In that capacity, he supervised vice presidents of human resources for Staples' four primary business units. Earlier in his career with Staples, he served in various roles including Vice President of Global HR Administration, Vice President of Worldwide HR Integration, and Vice President of European Strategy based in Belgium. Prior to joining Staples, Almeda held a management position with The Hertz Corporation, a $4.5 billion division of Ford Motor Company. Mr. Almeda is an active member of the Society for Human Resources Management (SHRM); serves on the Board of Directors of the New England Human Resources Association; and is an advisory board member of both The Workforce Institute at Kronos, and the Executive Program in Work-based Learning Leadership at the University of Pennsylvania/Wharton. A sought-after expert on HR issues, he has presented at or been published by organizations such as The Conference Board, Harvard Business School, and *CMO Magazine*. In addition to earning a bachelor's degree in marketing, Mr. Almeda also holds an MA in HR Management, and an EdD from The University of Pennsylvania's Wharton School/Graduate School of Education.

CHAPTER FOUR

DAN SCHAWBEL

Managing Partner, Millennial Branding, LLC

Founder, WorkplaceTrends.com

Dan Schawbel is the Founder of WorkplaceTrends.com, a research and advisory membership portal servicing HR professionals at companies including DreamWorks, Sodexo, Ericsson and Enterprise. He is also the Managing Partner of Millennial Branding, LLC, a Generation Y research and consulting firm, which has helped companies like American Express, NBC Universal, Ernst & Young, Deutsche Bank, Oracle, Fidelity and Monster better understand the Millennial Generation. He has published research studies that have been covered in media outlets including *The New York Times*, NBC, CNN, *USA Today* and *Men's Health*. The author of *The New York Times* and *The Wall Street Journal* bestselling book, *Promote Yourself: The New Rules for Career Success*, and the #1 international bestseller, *Me 2.0: 4 Steps to Building Your Future*, Mr. Schawbel is also a noted speaker and columnist at both *Time* and *Forbes*. He was named to the *Inc. Magazine's 30 Under 30 List* in 2010, *Forbes' 30 Under 30 List in 2012*, and *Business Insider's Top 40 Innovative People Under 40*. Mr. Schawbel holds a BS from Bentley University with a major in Marketing and a minors in IT and Management.

CHAPTER FIVE
SUSAN R. MEISINGER, SPHR, JD
Columnist, Speaker, Consultant
Former President and Chief Executive Officer,
Society for Human Resource Management (SHRM)

Susan R. Meisinger is the former President and Chief Executive Officer of the Society for Human Resource Management (SHRM). She served as Deputy Under Secretary for the Employment Standards Administration (ESA) in the U.S. Department of Labor. She also served as Special Legal Counsel for the Associated Builders and Contractors in Washington, D.C. A former board member of WFPMA, SHRM, HRCI, the Ethics Resource Center, and the Certified Financial Planner Board of Standards, Inc., she is also a former board member for BE&K, a billion dollar international design-build firm. Ms. Meisinger is a Fellow and member of the board of the National Academy of Human Resources (NAHR). She frequently serves as an expert on workplace and business issues in the national media. She co-wrote with former SHRM President and Chief Executive Officer Mike Losey, and University of Michigan's David Ulrich, *The Future of Human Resource Management*, published in 2005. Ms. Meisinger received a BA from Mary Washington College and a JD from the National Law Center of George Washington University. She is Certified as a Senior Professional in Human Resources from HRCI.

CHAPTER SIX
SHARLYN LAUBY, SPHR, CPLP
Author and Publisher, *HR Bartender*
President, ITM Group Inc.

Sharlyn Lauby is author of the blog *HR Bartender* and President of ITM Group Inc., a South Florida-based training and human resources consulting firm focused on helping companies retain and engage talent. Before starting ITM Group, Ms. Lauby was Vice President, Human Resources for Right Management Consultants, one of the world's largest organizational consulting firms. Known for expertise in bringing business solutions to reality and for exceptional program design skills, Ms. Lauby has created and implemented highly successful programs for employee retention, internal and external customer satisfaction, and leadership development. *Reuters, The New York Times,* ABC News, *TODAY, Readers Digest, Men's Health, Mashable* and *The Wall Street Journal* have sought out Ms. Lauby's expertise on topics related to human resources and the workplace. She launched *HR Bartender* in 2008 to provide a "friendly place for everyday workplace issues." The site has been recognized as one of the "Top 10 Business Blogs Worth Reading" by the Society for Human Resource Management (SHRM). She recently published her first book, *Essential Meeting Blueprints for Managers.* Ms. Lauby holds a BS in Political Science from the University of Central Florida.

CHAPTER SEVEN
JEANNE MEISTER
Partner, Future Workplace, LLC

Jeanne Meister is a Founding Partner of Future Workplace, a consulting firm dedicated to assisting organizations in re-thinking, re-imagining and re-inventing the workplace. Previously Ms. Meister was Vice President, Market Development at Accenture. She is the recipient of the Distinguished Contribution in Workplace Learning Award, which is given by the Association for Talent to one executive each year honoring their body of work. A contributor to *Forbes* and other publications, she has also appeared on numerous programs sharing future workplace best practices. In 2015, Ms. Meister was named a Top 50 influencer in corporate human resources and recruiting. Her latest book, co-written with Karie Willyerd, is titled *The 2020 Workplace: How Innovative Companies Attract, Develop, and Keep Tomorrow's Employees Today*. She is currently working with Kevin Mulcahy, Partner at Future Workplace LLC, on a new book which focuses on how organizations are preparing for the massive changes and disruptions in the workplace. She is a member of the Workforce Institute at Kronos, serves on the Executive Board for *CLO Magazine*, and sits on the Board of Directors of the Mahaiwe Center for Performing Arts in Great Barrington, MA.

KEVIN MULCAHY, MBA
Partner, Future Workplace, LLC

Kevin Mulcahy is a Partner at Future Workplace and teaches in the Entpreneurship Division at Babson College, where his classes focus on innovation, creativity, entrepreneurship, and new venture growth. He often conducts workshops and training sessions for governments, academic, and corporate audiences in Europe as well as in the Middle East, Caribbean, and Asia, where he discusses the workplace of the future, as well as applying scenario planning to "future proofing" HR strategies. Mr. Mulcahy headed up a practice at Fuld & Company, helping international and cross-functional teams gain insights and recommendations on market-entry strategy, market intelligence, and competitive intelligence. He also facilitated scenario planning and war-gaming exercises for Fortune 500 executives to align team members with long-term strategic initiatives. Mr. Mulcahy was Chief Executive Officer and founder of a multi-country global telecom reseller. He also served as a Corporate Strategist and Planner for Sprint Corporation and Sprint International, and was a Management Consultant at Gemini Consulting. He is currently co-authoring a book which will be published in 2016, with Jeanne Meister, Partner at Future Workplace. Mr. Mulcahy holds a BA in Management Science and Industrial Systems Studies from Trinity College in Dublin, Ireland, and an MBA in Strategy and Operations from Boston College. He is a dual U.S./Irish citizen.

CHAPTER 8

DAVID CREELMAN

Chief Executive Officer, Creelman Research

David Creelman is Chief Executive Officer of Creelman Research. He helps HR leaders identify, understand, and address important new issues in human capital management. His most recent book, which he wrote with John Boudreau, PhD and Ravin Jesuthasan, MBA, is titled *Lead the Work: Navigating a World Beyond Employment*. The book focuses on the future of work and has received plaudits from business leaders around the world. Mr. Creelman works closely with Wanda Wallace, PhD, on leadership transitions in knowledge-driven industries. He also partners with Carnegie-Mellon's Denise Rousseau, PhD, in leading a community of Fortune 500 companies on analytics and evidence-based management. A noted writer, researcher, and speaker, Mr. Creelman won the Walker Award for his work with Andrew Lambert on board oversight of human capital. He has spoken about reporting on human capital at the World Bank Headquarters in Paris, and has worked with the Etisalat Academy in Dubai. He is a member of the Workforce Institute at Kronos, and regularly conducts research for the Tokyo-based Works Institute. Mr. Creelman helped launch HR.com as Chief of Content and Research. He also worked for the Hay Group in Toronto and Kuala Lumpur, and taught an HR course at the University of Malaya. He holds an MBA from the University of Western Ontario, and a BSc Combined Honours in Chemistry and Biochemistry from McMaster.

CHAPTER NINE
CHINA GORMAN
Consultant, Speaker, and Author
Former Chief Executive Officer, Great Place to Work® Institute

China Gorman is a high-profile, successful global business executive in the competitive human capital management sector. She is well known for her tenure as Chief Executive Officer of the Great Place to Work® Institute, as well as for her years as Chief Operating Officer of the Society for Human Resource Management (SHRM), and President of Lee Hecht Harrison. A much sought-after consultant, speaker and writer who brings the C-Suite perspective to the challenges of building employee cultures for top performance and innovation, Ms. Gorman continues her work with organizations enhancing their brands and go-to-market strategies. Additionally, Ms. Gorman sits on the Executive Committee of the Board of Jobs for America's Graduates, and is on the advisory board for RiseSmart Inc. She also is a member of the Workforce Institute at Kronos, and is author of the popular blog *Data Point Tuesday*. Ms. Gorman is frequently quoted in *Fortune, Inc., The Huffington Post, Fast Company*, and *U.S. News & World Report*.